A LIFE IN CARTOONS

GILES:

A LIFE IN CARTOONS

The Authorised Biography of
Britain's Leading Cartoonist

Peter Tory

HEADLINE

First Published in 1992
by HEADLINE BOOK PUBLISHING PLC

10 9 8 7 6 5 4 3 2 1

The photographs in this book have been supplied by courtesy of Express Newspapers plc and Joan and Carl Giles, with the exception of p.56 (Lee Miller) and p.188 Jonathan Buckmaster.

British Library Cataloguing in Publication Data

Tory, Peter
Giles: Life in Cartoons – The Authorised Biography
of Britain's Leading Cartoonist
I. Title
741. 5092

ISBN 0-7472-0678-3

Designed by Penny Mills

Illustration reproduction by Koford, Singapore

Printed and bound in Great Britain by
Clays Ltd, St Ives PLC

HEADLINE BOOK PUBLISHING PLC
Headline House
79 Great Titchfield Street
London W1P 7FN

For Gwen

Acknowledgements

I would like to thank Carl Giles for all the time he generously gave to me, reminiscing about his life; I would also like to express my gratitude to Carl's wife Joan for her tireless and patient research; and thank both of them for their wonderful hospitality. My thanks also to Mark Burgess for his good-humoured assistance.

Contents

CHAPTER ONE

Giles Joins the *Daily Express*

For half a century people have asked: 'What's Giles like?' Such curiosity, expressed by three generations, has been entirely understandable. For Carl Giles has never, in newspaper or magazine, on radio or on television, on pavement or platform, successfully been interviewed. He has avoided publicity as a bat avoids daylight. Reporters who have attempted to probe have received little more than obstructive grunts and the only time anyone had the cheek to point a television camera at him he snarled at the lens and waved the intrusive contraption away with his cartooning pencil.

The following pages attempt to illuminate this shy subject, but for a brief introductory description it would seem appropriate to quote

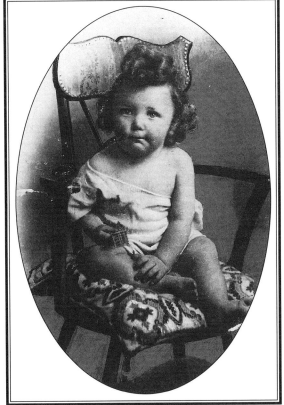

a man called John Gordon, the late celebrated editor of the *Sunday Express* and the figure who finally lured the young artist to Beaverbrook Newspapers, Carl's eventual home for fifty years.

'What is Giles like?' asked Gordon as the opening question to the introduction he composed for the first *Giles Annual* in 1947. Answering himself, he observed: 'Well, in a crowd he could hide as a man of no importance.

'He is slight, his fair hair is usually extremely untidy, he peers at you with a quizzical-puckered face, and he usually wears a pair of wide, uncreased baggy trousers, and often a leather golfing jacket. He certainly gives you no impression of being a great and successful man.

'He loathes town and prefers the quieter sociability of Ipswich. All

This is the earliest known photograph of young Ronald – as he was then – Giles. Later he was to be nicknamed 'Karlo' because of his cropped hair and his likeness, according to uncharitable friends, to horror film actor Boris Karloff. His later short, masculine hair-style may well have been a subconscious reaction to this very photograph. In any case, Karlo became Carl and, to Giles' eternal satisfaction, Ronald disappeared forever.

around that town I am told he is a familiar and well-liked figure as he moons about, seeking detail which one day will become a part of a cartoon.'

It was an agreeably sharp, newspaperman's description, though one or two of the details are a little awry. Socially, Carl doesn't 'moon' about, for this suggests someone, hands deep in pockets, kicking tin cans aimlessly about car parks. And the notion of the 'quieter sociability' of Ipswich is equally comical. Carl, in his social adventures up in Suffolk and thereabouts, kept much of East Anglia awake for nearly half a century. But more of that later in this chronicle. For the moment, it is 1943.

It was during the late summer of that year that the young Carl Giles was approached by the *Daily Express* and promised immortality, though he didn't quite see it in those grand terms. 'They bribed me,' he recalls. 'They stuck a cigar in my face and told me what was to be.'

The 27-year-old Carl had already established a reputation for brilliant work on *Reynolds News*, the left-wing Sunday journal owned by the Co-op. His talent was beginning to shine, each day brighter, in the uncertain and often inhospitable landscape of the newspaper industry. He was being noticed, especially by editors.

And thus it was that he was commanded into the presence of a senior representative of Lord Beaverbrook's *Daily Express,* a publication which sold nearly 3·5 million copies a day and which was regarded as the most influential popular newspaper of its generation.

The scene might have come from the pen of Giles himself.

We see the interior of an imposing dining hall, possibly in St James's. Ancient waiters shuffle and hover about the place. The features of some are hung low with years of anguished servitude and respect, the noses of others seek the rafters through decades of imagined superiority. Judges and elders glower down from portraits, in a corner a mouse totters towards the wainscoting with a burden of best Stilton retrieved from beneath the chair of a prematurely snoozing bishop. Through a vast window framed with heavy curtains, drawn into a low waist with tasselled cord, we see the club cat up a tree stalking an unwary pigeon. And so on.

At his table the fêted Giles sits with his eyes wide, a huge brandy balloon, golden with four-star cognac, wobbling in one hand, a cigar the size of a sausage dog in the other. Before him lie the remains of a glorious feast. Two empty champagne bottles tilt in an ice bucket. Opposite him is a large figure with fierce eyebrows and bulbous nose upon which the veins have long since abandoned themselves to the pressures of lunches such as this. A large index finger is held before the pale face of the young man with the cigar.

The caption might have read: 'Now, Mr Giles. What were you saying about not wanting to work for the *Daily Express?*'

Carl Giles accepted the job which, over the following fifty years, was to establish him as the greatest popular British cartoonist of all time. It was on 3 October 1943 that the first sketch was to appear for his new masters, in the *Sunday Express.*

Giles, overnight, was established. His Midas salary was twenty guineas a week. However, the exact manner of his arrival at this prestigious new job and his initial response to the move over to Fleet Street from his beloved *Reynolds News*, tucked away at the end of Gray's Inn Road near King's Cross, was recalled rather differently by John Gordon.

'I will tell you frankly that the transfer was not an easy matter. Geniuses, as everyone like myself who has to drive a team of them knows, are "Kittle Cattle", as they say in Scotland. Sometime you coax them, sometimes you drive them, sometimes they cry on your knee, sometimes they drive you to almost crying on theirs. But by and large they have one attribute in common. At the start, at least, whatever change may come over them later, they are not susceptible to money persuasion. You can't bribe them.

'Giles was like that. He was making very little money

'Hermann—you've left that verdammt door open again.' Sunday Express, Oct. 3rd, 1943

Here, in the first Giles cartoon which was to appear in the Sunday Express *or* Daily Express, *Hitler is blaming Hermann Goering, his Luftwaffe chief, for letting the Russians in through the back door, the Eastern Front. Note Mussolini is at the end of a dog leash. Also Goering playing with his train set.*

'Never mind about it not being 'arf wot we're giving them—let's git 'ome.'

Sunday Express, Feb. 27th, 1944

Giles, according to his old editor Arthur Christiansen, had not been too happy during his early period at the Express. *But he was soon cheered up by the increasing flood of affectionate letters from the public. Here is an example of a Giles London-at-war cartoon, published early in 1944, which the* Sunday Express *readers adored.*

indeed. I took the lid off Aladdin's cave and let him peep in. All he kept on saying was: "I am very happy where I am. I would be very unhappy if I changed."

'Well, they say water wears away a stone. Certainly, it took much water and other liquids to wear down this particular stone, but in the end, as I determined it should be in the beginning, I transferred it from the other brook to mine.

'It would probably be true to say, and I think Giles would agree with it, that having made the change he became for a time a very unhappy man. He missed the old familiar faces and the old comfortable setting. He was uncertain, diffident and thoroughly miserable.

'Then all of sudden he changed. The old certainty of touch returned. The sad grey eyes began to twinkle again behind the heavy spectacles. One day I heard him laugh uproariously at one of his own jokes.

'What caused the change? The usual thing. Readers had begun to write to him in masses telling him how much they liked him.'

'Well—what are YOU waiting for?'   Daily Express, April 19th, 1944

D-Day approaches over the Channel. Happy Dutchmen look out to sea. One looks at his watch. The invasion was seven weeks away.

Thereafter, for half a century, with only the occasional break brought about by the inconveniences of war and, in later days, ill health, Carl produced three drawings a week, one for the *Sunday* and two for the *Daily*.

His most celebrated and loved creation, the appalling Family, headed by the tyrannical matriarch, Grandma, a figure whom some falsely believed Carl had based on Lord Beaverbrook himself, slowly evolved, finally to terrorise suburban England in days of peace.

'What a beautiful morning! It wouldn't surprise me if you get your invasion today.'

Daily Express, May 4th, 1944

D-Day nears and Mussolini, in his nightcap, has sprung from his cot beside Hitler's four-poster with a merry thought for the day. Hitler has one horrified eye open.

16

'Himmel! Tourists!'

Sunday Express, June 11th, 1944

The Allied Forces have landed. Giles has been at the Express *for nine months. He is loving it. And he's now a national figure.*

It's quicker by rail.

Sunday Express, Aug. 5th, 1945

Peace descends on the world. Or does it? Here is the first appearance of the Giles 'Family'. They are in prototype form and were to grow and develop into a kind of anarchic suburban royalty. The country would, eventually, look to them for a sense of continuity. Some feel they have done a rather better job.

'Bang! And there goes the officers' mess.'   *Sunday Express, Nov. 5th, 1944*

Few things can be funnier for a Giles tommy than to see the officers' mess being blown up.

But this was war. And, throughout, Carl found himself at the sharp end, often underneath the bombs and, in Europe, frequently in range of the bullets.

Thus his characters were the bus drivers and cabbies of London, the florid-faced squires who were forced to accommodate evacuee children in their stately piles, the nurses and policemen, the station masters, the air raid wardens, the sergeant majors and buffoonish brigadiers, cheeky-featured tommies, German soldiers and, most famous of all, perhaps, the GIs. Carl saw the conflict under the Blitz and also, as official war artist for the *Daily Express*, in many parts of Europe. He was flown into Arnhem with the Coldstream Guards and sat drawing for his office amidst the blaze, dust and rubble of battle.

A cartoon of that time shows him, a ludicrously unmilitary figure in ill-fitting battle tunic with the word 'press' drawn on his bottom, sketching at his pad, perched on an ammunition box, while two privates stroll past. One of them observes: 'I'd sooner they sent us a few pullovers instead of cartoonists.'

Carl avoided depicting the despair and the pain. His was always a cheery view. But he didn't draw heroes either. 'Well, they weren't, most of them, were they?' he observed.

He recalls: 'I tried to have fun with the drawings. I would have a group of soldiers looking down the street – you know, where there were shells of houses and so on – and there would be a big explosion. The caption would be: "BANG. There goes the officers' mess." That kind of thing.'

Another drawing of the time shows a British soldier in the ruin of a Dutch home turning on the tap of a shattered sink which is hanging from the wall. What is funny, of course, is the British irony. The tommy knew that there wouldn't be any hot water but went through the nonsense of turning it on.

'I'd sooner they sent us a few pullovers instead of cartoonists.'

Sunday Express, Nov. 22nd, 1944

Giles is sent to war in Europe as the Express's *official war cartoonist. He was unable to serve in the forces because of an injury he received in a serious motor-bike accident at the age of nineteen. He was practically deaf in one ear. He happily went off to draw instead of fight but Giles was very conscious that the military might not quite see the point of such a figure in the midst of their more appropriate endeavours.*

'Just as I expected—no hot water.'

Daily Express, Oct. 17th, 1944

No water! Not that he really expected there to be. Note the detail in the pouches and straps, the broken beams and shell marks.

'Well—how's Mr Invincible this morning?'   Sunday Express, Sept. 10th, 1944

The Allies prevail. They sweep across Belgium. They have already opened a second front in France. In this splendid cartoon a British tommy passes the time of day with a disconsolate German.

'Your Missus would give you "Vive La Belgique" if she was to come round the corner.'

Daily Express, Oct. 11th, 1944

Giles celebrates the liberation of Belgium. He was there himself with the Allies.

'Pfennig for your thoughts, mein Herren?'

Daily Express, Feb. 27th, 1945

Giles had enormous fun with the collapse of the Third Reich. The poster of Hitler shows Giles' great gift as a caricaturist.

'Sh!—We're listening to Churchill.'

Sunday Express, June 5th, 1945

No collection of Giles' wartime cartoons would be complete without one featuring his famous Japanese soldiers. They all had identical mouths, like motor car grilles. Note the painstaking contrast in the uniforms of Japanese and tommy; every detail is accurate to the smallest button.

Carl was able to make everyone laugh among the destruction, especially at the activities of the ordinary infantryman whom he so loved.

As the war progressed, Carl achieved glorious success in reducing such monsters as Hitler, Mussolini and Japan's Tojo to figures of absurd dimension and clownish demeanour. His favourite subject of the three was Mussolini and Carl must have been one of the few people in the world to have felt a deep sense of personal loss when he was executed.

'I hated to see old Musso go,' he said. 'He was half my bloody stock-in-trade.'

Indeed, after Il Duce retreated to Hitler's protective custody in northern Italy he became a regular knock-about comedy star in Giles' daily lampoon. Seen as a small, stupid country relative of Der Führer, he was always underfoot and embarrassing his host at important parties.

Carl found rich humour in the war, although he experienced some terrifying moments during the height of the German bombing raids on London, as did his fiancée, Joan Clarke, a first cousin, childhood companion and, eventually, teenage sweetheart whom he married in 1942.

Joan lived in Great Percy Street and Carl worked half a mile away opposite the end of Gray's Inn Road. Both addresses were on the lethal line formed by six main-line railway stations, Liverpool Street, King's Cross, St Pancras, Euston, Marylebone and Paddington. It was a principal run for Goering's pilots. It was a bomb alley.

This was the area of London where Carl and Joan had been brought up together and where they had gone to school. Until a year or so earlier it had been a jostling, cheerful, villagy kind of a place, just north and east of the heart of the city; now, in the first real bombing war of history, it was the citizen's front line.

CHAPTER TWO

Childhood and Chalkie

Carl was born next to a pub at the Angel, Islington, during the First World War on 29 September 1916. The joyous din of carousing and wassail must have made an instantly agreeable impact, for Carl was to adore pubs throughout his life. His place of birth, much to his quiet pleasure, is now honoured with a tavern named after him – The Giles. The pub's sign bears a ferocious picture of Grandma.

Giles' name has always caused a puzzle. Many have assumed that Giles is his Christian name. It is his surname. And 'Carl' isn't his natural first name. Giles was christened Ronald.

In his young days as an artist he took to wearing his hair, once unkempt, very short and cropped. His friends suggested he looked like Boris Karloff, the Hollywood-based English actor who made a career for himself playing Franken-stein's monster opposite Bela Lugosi.

Carl's chums started to call him Carlo – or Karlo – as it would have been spelt – and eventually Carl. So he

Grandpa Giles was a jockey who rode for Edward VII. He died at the age of 53 in April 1910, six years before Carl was born. His premature death was brought about, it was thought, by the constant battle to keep his weight down.

became Carl Giles. He has always rather liked the name and has certainly never been happy with the idea of 'Ron'. Ronald, in the end, simply died away.

Carl's arrival into the world was within a day or so of the sort of event which would have made the subject, some years later, of a very jolly Giles cartoon. Not many miles away an Essex special constable had been getting dressed when he heard the sinister droning of a German Zeppelin. The sound stopped abruptly and moments later there was an explosion. The constable, shirt-tails flying and his whistle between his lips, ran down the road and met the airship's whole crew strolling towards him. Despite the fact that he was greatly out-numbered he apprehended the lot and marched them into custody. He was quite unperturbed by the moment of excitement, according to a report of the time, for 'this afternoon he was back on duty directing traffic in his home town'. The place was Cockfosters.

Carl's grandfather had been a jockey who rode for

Edward VII and his father ran a tobacconist's shop in the Barbican. It was a small and well-patronised emporium of glorious tobacco smells, the scents of every blend imaginable drifting about a neat row of black barrels which stood, in an impressive row, on the floor in front of the counter. Men puffed away and sampled the odours and treated the place very much as a club. Carl's father was a conscientious, decent and much-liked man.

Young Carl, an extrovert, cheerful, bespectacled, flaxen-haired, mischievous child, went to the local Barnsbury Park School. He remembers it as a 'large red box in a square of asphalt'. He wasn't academically of much consequence, but he could draw like a dream from the moment he was able to hold a pencil; not that such an ability was the slightest bit impressive to anyone at such a school and at such a time. Art, like dancing and designing frocks and creating pastry dainties, was regarded with some contempt. Said Carl, who has always retained friendly traces of his working-class London accent: 'It was no good talking about being an artist. What was an artist? There was mention from time to time of commercial art, but that was about it.'

So Carl sat in his class, the sunshine slanting through the swirling chalk dust, doodling like a genius in private corners of his exercise book and regarding with immense distaste the master who presided over those few years of early education, an unsmiling, formidable fellow called Mr Chalk. It was upon Mr Chalk, of course, that Carl based one of his most gloriously successful characters, the vinegary schoolmaster, Chalkie. Never in the history of the classroom did one small boy enjoy such a terrible, fearful revenge on his teacher.

'He was a tall man, like a skeleton, and he had a head like a skull,' recalls Carl. 'He lived in the country, Potters Bar – that was the country in those days – and he was always going on about it. And he was always going on about his daughters – we used to mimic what we thought they were like. But what one really remembers about him was not so much the cane but his sarcasm. He was a sarcastic bugger.

'Mind you, you knew about it all right when he used the cane. You got six on the palm and you couldn't use your hand for weeks. It was the same with the girls. And in those days you didn't go running home to tell your mother. If you did that you'd just get caned again.

'The funny thing was that he had a good reputation. He had been a head teacher.'

Carl, like all of his schoolfriends, was terrified of this ex-headmaster who was now teaching general subjects to a mixed class of forty as a last offering to Academia before retirement.

Carl himself was not exactly the kind of pupil who brought serenity to the quieter, more contemplative moments of a schoolmaster's existence. Just as the tyrannical Mr Chalk and his reign of fear gave Giles one of his most enduring characters, so the behaviour of the young Giles, and his chums, was undoubtedly the inspiration for those little monsters of his cartoons who shot arrows at the neighbour's parrot and attached fireworks to the cat under Grandma's chair. For lively testimony to this we need go no further than Carl's sister, Eileen.

Eileen was six years younger than Carl and was the uncomplaining victim, at his hands, of the most relentless and heartless persecution.

The cruelties, in particular, involved the household mangle, that old-fashioned but very effective pre-spin-drier device which pressed water out of fabric. It consisted of two rollers between which the washing was passed at the turn of a large handle. It was doubtless used by some youngsters, pressing little pink fingers into service, as it were, as a dreadful form of physical torture. But Carl's application of the contraption was far more subtle. He simply wound between the rollers Eileen's dolls and teddy bears. As each now cuddly bear or pink-cheeked doll made its appearance at Christmas or on birthdays, it would soon be put, to the soundless

'Never mind what the archbishop will say—here comes Chalkie.' Daily Express, Jan. 16th, 1958

Enter Chalkie. Mr Chalk was the sarcastic tyrant of a schoolmaster who terrorised Giles and his classmates at Barnsbury Park School, Islington. He is the only Giles character who is drawn, accurate in every detail, from someone who actually existed. Giles has spent a lifetime enjoying the most terrible schoolboy revenge. Here, the Archbishop of Canterbury's warnings concerning test tube babies are nothing to the fear that stalks the chemistry lab.

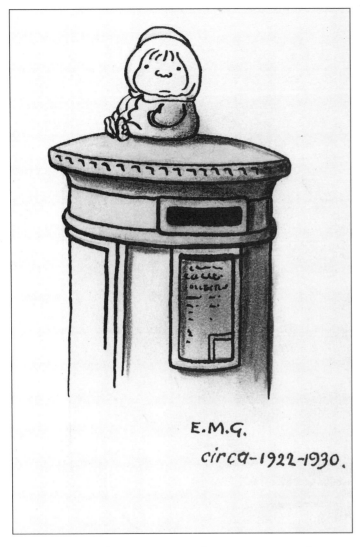

E.M.G.

circa-1922-1930.

Giles' sister Eileen, six years his junior, was the mute victim to her older brother's tyranny. All her teddy bears, golliwogs and tubes of paint were put through mother's mangle. Eileen herself, when Giles required her to be kept out of the way, was placed on a red pillar box. She would sit there silently for long periods. Giles warned her that if she told their mother then God, who was a personal friend of his, would tell him. Note the sinister caption under Eileen's initials.

horror of its innocent owner, through the household wringer. 'She never told anyone,' recalls Carl, still hugely entertained by the memories, 'because I made her believe that I was a friend of God, and that if she told Mum, God would tell me.

'Those dolls and teddy bears and things, all flat, looked really hideous after they'd been through that thing. And I remember Eileen had an enormous box of flat tubes of paint. They'd all been through the mangle.'

Carl has a most infectious chuckle which feeds on itself. His recollections concerning Eileen cause huge merriment.

'When we played I didn't want to be bothered by her so I put her up on top of one of those red pillar boxes in the street. It was too high for her to get down. She just sat there with her flat teddy bear. She never objected. She never even cried. She knew God was watching.'

Mr Chalk, whose first name appears never to have been known, was evidently a fine teacher. He was, recalls Carl, an Oxbridge man and a professor. Carl admits to holding him in great respect and at times, however briefly, some affection.

'There was a kind of warmth about him,' says Carl. 'And he taught me more than anyone else ever did. He was very hot on geometry and I still use his method of finding the centre of a circle today.'

Certainly, there is little doubt that Mr Chalk was very much at the top of his league in terms of his ability to quell and control a host of children.

'His object in life,' says Carl, 'was to be frightening. When we came creeping in to the classroom a bit late he would take his glasses off and say with that terrible sarcasm: "How nice of you to join us." ·

'On the first day of term my little mob – a real dreadful lot – would come in and sit in a gang, clustered in the same area at the back of the class. There was Mott, Gomm and Fletcher and Georgie Smith. My God, we were frightened of Smith. He lived in a rougher road than I did. They styled you by the street you came from.

**'That's my Chalkie—rest of the school get sent home because of the fuel shortage
and we have to hop round the room to keep warm.'**

Daily Express, Jan. 12th, 1972

Chalkie again. Here he copes with the long hard winter of 1972, a season of misery brought about by striking miners.

'Chalkie would look at us all and he'd take his glasses off and hold them up and slowly clean them. "Oh, yes, yes, yes, yes, yes, yes, yes, yes," he would say. "How very nice. Are you all comfortable?" His voice was so silky and friendly. Then he would shout: "GET UP!" And we would all jump. And then he would redistribute us round the class.'

Carl also has an example of Mr Chalk's startlingly contrived spitefulness.

'I was good at the violin,' he recalls. 'I liked it. And I played in the school orchestra.

'One day we were to give a concert to the governors of the board. I was in the classroom and I had my violin under the desk and we could all hear the orchestra

'You are all very fortunate that you live in a country with less stringent laws about literature than Iran.'

Daily Express, Feb. 21st, 1989

Chalkie at his best/worst. Look at the languid pose. With what clarity Giles remembers him! He was responding to the news from Teheran that Salman Rushdie had been sentenced to death for upsetting Iranians. Note the little bespectacled chap who is one up from the bottom left-hand corner. Could that be Giles?

tuning up in the assembly hall. I was too terrified to ask Chalkie if I could get up and leave the class. I wanted to say: "Can I please go into the hall, sir?" And he knew.

'The headmaster then came in and asked: "Where's Giles? He should be playing in the concert." And Chalkie said: "What concert? I don't know anything about a concert." So when I went out I had to go up on the stage and tune my violin all by myself when the others had finished. The instrument was flat for the whole recital and the conductor kept glaring at me.'

Carl also tells a tale of Chalkie which he suggests shows evidence of a kindness existing in almost equal parts with cruelty.

'We had a flower show in the school. It was one of those things where all the parents come to see the exhibition.

'I had grown a sweet william in a little pot – a tiny little pot. It was just poking up out of the soil. I was very proud of it and kept walking round it and looking at it.

'One day after prayers we were in class and Chalkie looked at my little thing and said: "Ladies and gentlemen, we have *an* horticulturist in our midst" – he loved saying an horticulturist – "It is Mr Giles." And there was my little sweet william poking up. And then he said: "I must show Mr Giles what a sweet william should really look like." Then he brought out this beautiful flower which he had grown in Potters Bar. He handed it to me and said: "You can take this home with you."

'I took it home and told everyone it was mine. They were all impressed. Chalkie had done me a kindness.

'But on another occasion I had won the school knock-out draughts competition. Chalkie was in charge. And it was discovered that there was no prize. So Chalkie gave me a new tennis ball. What was the point of a tennis ball? It wasn't even presented in any way. He could be a sod.'

And then there were the cigarettes. Carl had rather unwisely brought to school, from his father's shop, a tin of fifty bogus, entirely harmless 'fags' which were used simply for display and advertising purposes. There was no tobacco in them. However, the attractive packaging and appealing quantity, plus the tight look of all those snug ciggies as wicked as rifle bullets in a box, had proved irresistible to Carl.

The long index finger of Mr Chalk, whose death's head countenance had suddenly appeared above Carl, prodded towards the bulge in Carl's pocket. Mr Chalk's palm turned upwards and the extended digit curled in a chilling gesture of command. The 'cigarettes' were placed in his hand. Not a word was said.

'I'm sure I didn't even tell him that they weren't real,' says Carl. 'I was just too frightened of him. Anyway he went round and told my father and must have learned that they were fake. But he never said anything to me.'

There is no doubt that the schoolmaster, whose profoundly unpleasant qualities hid a strange kind of nobility, had a lasting effect on this particular pupil. Carl's recollections of over sixty years ago are as vivid as if he were speaking of yesterday. And Mr Chalk has remained with him, and with us; a ghost with a skull face and long bony fingers and a terrible way with sarcasm.

Carl, wearied by the restrictions of education, left school at the age of fourteen.

He almost immediately found employment in Wardour Street as an office boy and, to his subsequent delight, an animator on cartoon films. 'I got ten shillings a week, rising to twelve shillings, but it was wonderful. We worked long, long hours, often up to midnight, but we didn't mind.'

At this time, Carl and pretty young Joan Clarke, whose father was circulation manager of the *Evening News*, were inseparable friends. There was no thought that they would ever be more than that. They were, after all, first cousins.

'We just all went out together and went to parties together, I with my boy friend and Carl with his girl friend,' said Joan. 'I really can't remember when our friendship developed into anything else. Carl was just one of the family. But I do remember him as a young devil, along with my brother Terry who was his great friend. I don't mean that they were wicked, so much, but they just got up to tricks all the time. They were always making people laugh. Carl was one of the family, really. He was just always around.'

Carl admits, however, to a retrospective jealousy when he ferried Joan and some boy friend of hers to the local park after work one day and collected them after dark, driving the young man home to South London.

'He was a prat,' recalls Carl in one of those spirited moments of irritation.

By the age of eighteen, Carl had moved from Wardour Street to work at Elstree for the renowned film-maker, Alexander Korda. There he was one of the animators on a full-length cartoon feature called *The Fox Hunt*, a work which Korda hoped would establish him as a British Disney. The project was never properly completed, though the film was shown, briefly, at London's Curzon cinema. It was soon forgotten.

The Korda office moved to nearby Isleworth. And it was at about this time that Carl, who was to have a long and expensive romance with fast and glamorous machinery, acquired a Panther 600 motorcycle. It was kicked into action by a violent thrust of the right heel and to ride the thing you wore large gauntlets and goggles. It made a devil of a noise and children, nannies, dogs and tortoises scattered at its coming.

His affair with the Panther ended abruptly one day when he was rounding a corner at speed, head down, lips drawn back by the slipstream, his bellowing machine banking like an aeroplane. He did not see the large lorry, probably full of chickens, travelling towards him outside the studio gates. Carl hurtled into the truck's grille head on.

He remembers nothing. But he was incapacitated for nearly a year. He had fractured his skull and, almost as seriously, done grave damage to his drawing hand, in particular his thumb.

Giles described Joan as 'the prettiest girl I had ever seen'. She is a first cousin. The couple never had children. Giles and Joan grew up together and cannot remember precisely when childhood friendship turned to love. But it certainly did. Joan is strong, patient, practical, charming and courageous. Giles has been a lucky man.

It was Joan who comforted him in his plaster, wire-frame contraptions and straps when he was in hospital following his accident.

Joan, so much a recognisable product of the thirties and forties, is one of those quiet, serene heroines who can be imagined standing on a dockside in the war or on a station platform as the troops go off to Southampton, amidst the human, tearful jostle of emotional departure and the inconsiderate steam of belching locomotives. She is the one to the side of the barrier, pretty, pale and undemonstrative, who slowly raises a hand in farewell and doesn't weep.

CHAPTER THREE

Giles the War Artist

Carl wasn't a soldier. He is an artist. An often appallingly crotchety man, a joy when inspired and wonderful company when in full merry flow at a party; a fascinating, charming and funny observer of the way of the world, a magnificent host who insists on pleasure: a sometimes dark and snarling beast – he enjoys an occasional shout of rage, a sudden, ferocious burst of bad language – and a genius.

It is difficult to imagine a more suitable partner and lifetime supporter for such a man than the practical, strong, unwavering, deeply loving, courageous Joan Clarke. Almost from childhood she has managed Carl and filed his work and kept him organised; fed him, forgiven him and, above all, loved him with an incredible

depth of devotion and loyalty.

In these later days the couple have known, in terms of health if not material comforts, very hard times indeed. Carl is confined to a wheelchair and is utterly dependent on Joan.

'JOAN!' he bellows. The tiles stir. Birds rise from a neighbouring spinney. And from somewhere in the house we hear the reassuring 'Coming, Carl.'

Carl puts his view of his lady, as usual, into a bright visual context: 'She transports me.'

'Why?' he was asked.

'Because she is my elevator.'

Two years after his accident, in 1937, Carl was working at a studio in Ipswich. His brother Bert, who was ten years older, was employed in a garment factory in London and was involved in an industrial accident, badly injuring his knee.

There was no photographic record of Giles' and Joan's wedding. The snaps didn't come out. Such things happened in those days. But here is a picture taken on top of the Daily Express *building in Fleet Street of the couple at the time that Giles was sent off to war. Joan looks proud. Giles looks as though he could have gone over the top with a fixed bayonet. But the only weapons in his kitbag were sketch pad and pencil.*

The wound became gangrenous and Bert died. Their mother was distraught. Carl moved immediately back to London to be with her. And almost immediately was offered employment at the left-wing Sunday paper, *Reynolds News*.

The war came. And Carl, whose office at King's Cross was within short walking distance of Joan's home in Great Percy Street, started to stay there with Joan and her mother. The couple still, today, insist that they cannot remember when their relationship developed into more than cousinly friendship. In any event, they were married in 1942 at St John's Church, East Finchley.

'Well, Madam, if you have definitely decided not to vote for me what am I doing nursing your baby?'
Sunday Express, Feb. 12th, 1950

Each Giles cartoon is like a still from a moving sequence. Giles had been an animator. This horrifying though, nevertheless, hilarious sketch seems to have a life both before and after. Here you can almost see what led to the incident and can certainly imagine, with dreadful clarity, what follows it. Giles has frozen the moment as if he'd stopped the film. This sketch also illustrates the dark side of his humour.

37

There is no record of the event, for the photographs taken by 'someone called Joe from *Reynolds News*' didn't come out. The honeymoon was at the Great White Horse Hotel in Ipswich. The pair had to travel there by train, despite Carl's love of motor cars and by now increasingly healthy financial circumstances, because of petrol rationing.

Says Joan: 'We stayed in the Dickens suite. I remember it had two four-poster beds.'

The idea of two four-poster beds, curious by any standards of accommodation, has more than an agreeable touch of Giles lunacy about it.

And so it was that a year later, in 1943, Carl joined the *Daily Express*.

From that day – and for the next fifty years – Carl Giles gave the world the most gloriously colourful,

'Apart from the 209,000,000 Russians watching the Trooping on TV, I shall be watching—so this year we'll try it without half of you falling feet over head.'

Daily Express, May 16th, 1961

See the detail on the rifles, the shine on the boots. You expect, at any moment, a guardsman to fall over in the picture before you. This cartoon followed news that the Russians had finally acquired television.

'If you saw Fred's Missus you'd understand him being in love with his tram.'

Sunday Express, July 6th, 1952

Another example of the film-like quality of Giles' work is this cartoon which marked the news that London's tramways were to be closed. The weeping figure could easily have been Giles himself. He loved trams.

uncannily true, scalpel-sharp and brightly living cast of recognisable characters which can ever have grown from the tip of an artist's pen.

His style was revolutionary, for he drew into his cartoons an almost photographic reality. This was unknown.

A commentator observed in the late forties: 'The secret of Giles' cartoons lies in his movie training – his training in animation with Korda and people.

'He draws in a panel shaped like a movie screen.

'His carefully built background architecture is as authentic as a naturalistic stage setting. His characters are placed on stage with directorial skill.

'When he shows his drawings to friends he delights in telling them what the characters have been doing up to the moment he has chosen to draw them – and what happens to them afterwards.

'In dreaming up a cartoon situation he imagines a

complete dramatic sequence and orders his brainchildren to act it out. When they come to the climactic moment, Giles says mentally "Hold it" and proceeds to draw them.'

Carl's attention to detail was incredibly painstaking. Every soldier's uniform was accurate in every particular. He worked for many hours on each drawing. It was said at the time that a group of green soldiers on the Rhine once bagged a Gestapo general after quick reference to a Giles cutting showing a member of the Geheimstaatspolizei in uniform.

Look at Carl's sailing boats, too, and anyone who has put to sea under canvas will know that each line and halyard, each cleat and stanchion is exactly as it should be.

His was – is – a real world. Britain is a real land, a place of grocers' shops, bookies and suburban gardens and living rooms. Carl's work was a kind of *cinéma-vérité* of cartoonery. And his work always brought laughter.

He was neither sentimental nor malicious. There is great warmth in his drawings, even when his characters

Giles at the wheel of his beloved Jaguar XK120. He raced it at Silverstone in the fifties. Now it gathers rust and dust in his garage. Giles occasionally opens the door and simply gazes at his beloved motor. A farmer offered him £250,000 for it. He said he would sell his farm to raise the money. Giles declined.

are monsters. 'For me at any rate,' says Carl, 'I like to think that there is even a certain warmth to Grandma. And Chalkie.'

Giles, above all, displayed a touching affection and understanding of his country and countrymen. His was – and is – a decent, funny England.

Carl's politics are a surprise. He almost became, in those days at *Reynolds News,* a communist.

He still claims that he is well left of Left, though, on visiting his splendid home and studying a life dedicated to fun and impressive material ownership, it is difficult to find a great deal of evidence for it.

'Well, I'm a Bentley-driving socialist,' he says with one of those sudden smiles and without further explanation. The unspoken conclusion, perhaps, is that everyone should be allowed to drive a Bentley. But it's not just his Bentley Mulsanne Turbo (price £70,000); there's also the Jaguar XK120 that he raced at Silverstone in 1952, the shiny Range Rover, his beautiful farm and, until recently, his

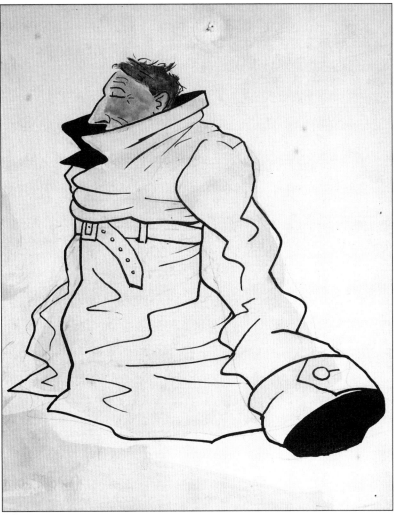

This departure from the Giles style is a tribute to one of Giles' heroes when he was cartoonist on Reynolds News. *It shows Giles' colleague on the paper, Monty Slater, a well-known communist writer of the time and the man who, in 1945, wrote the libretto for Benjamin Britten's opera,* Peter Grimes.

yacht, a Nicholson 38. With great sadness he had to sell his Nicholson, certainly the most precious of all his grand acquisitions.

So what can be the explanation for his left-wing convictions? His father, after all, was a traditional Stanley Holloway, working-class Tory. He was a royalist whose walls were covered with pictures of Queen Victoria and Edward VII, and whose sympathies during the General Strike were entirely with the military personnel who had to keep the buses going.

In part, the answer is simple. At Reynolds News Carl came under the influence and, finally, under the political wing of two of the most celebrated communist commentators of the day, Alan Hutt and Monty Slater. The former was a columnist and expert on printing. He was more communist than Stalin, says Carl, but 'an honest one'.

Carl recounts with affection one particular anecdote which illustrates the man.

'I had borrowed some money from him and had

Giles even managed, on at least one occasion, to make the Russians laugh. During the winter battles for Stalingrad, one of his cartoons was reprinted in the Soviet Union as a billboard. In a snowbound forest, Soviet guerrillas watch a bizarre procession approaching. Through the trees comes a little old peasant grandmother pulling a rope, at the end of which a dozen Nazi prisoners are trussed.

Grandma, holding up a deprecatory hand, says: 'It's nothing, Tovarishi, you should have seen the one that got away.'

been rather slow in paying it back. Then one day he wrote me a note which said: "Loath as I am to raise the raucous cry of the market – what about my fifty quid?"'

Slater, who also had a column on *Reynolds*, wrote the libretto to Benjamin Britten's opera *Peter Grimes*. They were men of intellect, culture and charm. To Carl, they became heroes.

At lunchtime they would all go out, in the tradition of Fleet Street, and talk animatedly about the ways of the world. They gathered at a restaurant and drinking place on the corner of Holborn called Musso's.

'The Russians had been through Stalingrad, showing magnificent resolve and bravery,' says Carl. 'They had been all but destroyed and rebuilt their army and air force. It was very moving.'

Carl's politics are the politics of the heart and soul, rather than the result of intellectual agonising. Study his work and you will see that he identifies with the ordinary bloke, the ordinary family, the unpretentious,

'Fall out the man who said "It's a fiddle!" when the Sergeant Major drew a leave pass.'
Daily Express, Dec. 7th, 1944

A line of tommies queue for a leave pass. Look at the splendidly cheeky features of the foot-soldiers and compare them with the absurd faces of the officers. Note the sergeant major's moustache and chin.

'If this new attack on the Western Front means the end of the war, I suppose we shall be losing our little evacuee friends, your lordship.'

Sunday Express, March 4th, 1945

Meanwhile on the home front the country's squires were being required to act as host to evacuee children from the cities, particularly from London. Note the dog regarding the firework!

the unstuffy, the unsnooty. In many respects he appears anti-authoritarian. (Memories of Mr Chalk.)

He doesn't mind the copper on the beat too much, not even the sergeant, but he's not keen on the inspector. Ask certain newspaper management men. He has given them a dreadful time. They are insensitive wretches who do not really understand him or his work. They are figures who are preoccupied with schedules and balance sheets and train times and office hours and 'new ideas' and budgets. They don't comprehend and they are there to frustrate and irritate and not get the point.

Usually good-natured, though damnably prickly and difficult on occasions, the other things which put Carl into a state of high irritation include humbug, any suggestion of elitism, snobbishness or what he perceives to be Tory attitudes.

Basically, he doesn't like the idea of Tories at all, even though he has hobnobbed with them, on and off, for most of his life. On the subject of Margaret Thatcher, for example, he could become almost incoherent with anger – a trembling flute of champagne in his hand at the bar of the Savoy.

His always hilarious depiction in his drawings of the difference between the classes is the best illustration of his attitude to the subject. Examine the features of the tommy, the foot soldier, and compare them to the colonel's. The one displays a lopsided, cheeky face, the other has no chin at all, just a long sharp nose from which is suspended an absurd moustache and set of prominent teeth. A ninny.

Did he draw such figures of authority with amusement or distaste? 'A combination of the two,' says Carl.

The sergeant major is all right, of course. Here is a figure of unshakable integrity, authority and indestructibility, the possessor of a massive chin – eyes obscured by the peak of the cap – a powerful chest, and a spine constructed of that sturdy piece of gun-cleaning equipment, the ramrod. The major, on the other hand,

has a cruel, arrogant face. The brigadier, if that's what he is, is a moustachioed blimp.

Carl is equally at home in the public bar or the saloon bar. But it is with the public bar, perhaps, that he might wish to be associated. He lights up to the cry: ''Ere, Carl, mate, what yer havin'?'

Today, he sets out on regular lunchtime jaunts to the outskirts of Ipswich to settle, secure in his wheelchair, with half a pint of ginger beer in the company of artisans.

One morning he was in a favourite bar, built into the side of Ipswich's football terraces, when a fellow, who could only have been a gypsy, approached us with one of those pugilists' belts, a huge affair made heavy with every kind of brass shield and bare-knuckled fairground disc of honour imaginable.

The man was plainly drunk and engaged Carl in a long and incomprehensible diatribe. Carl nodded intently and chuckled quietly.

'You see, Carl, me old pal, what you've got to understand is this...'

'Oh really,' said Carl. 'Ha, ha. Yes, quite. Uh huh. I see.'

Any witness might have assumed that here was a friendship of some maturity. However, when the chap had lurched out with his belt, Carl looked at the barman with great amusement and enquired: 'Who was he?'

Whoever he was he might certainly, on another day, have featured in a Giles cartoon. He would have turned up, most probably, as a Romany character on Epsom Common during Derby Day.

Carl continues to be roguish with barmaids. He twinkles at them from his wheelchair. They appear to love it. After a while he will say: 'Hey, Peter, have you met my favourite niece?' Or: 'What do you think of my nurse?' The success of his charm on women has always been spectacular. It remains so. As his friend, comedian Michael Bentine, says: 'Carl manages in a quite extraordinary manner to combine being a ladies' man

*'I said to my wife, "Florrie, old dear, why don't you go in for it?" Then I said,
"No, old darling, you're too busy."'*

Daily Express, April 27th, 1971

Giles has spent much of his life in pubs. He enjoyed them for the rich cast of characters as much as for the booze. Curiously, he often drew barmaids in a rather unflattering

light. You would expect to see those alluring Giles creatures with big bosoms and tight sweaters. But they were usually more homely ladies.

and man's man. I've never seen it achieved so successfully before.' But he's happiest to be one of the lads.

So the people's journal, *Reynolds News*, was a comfortable home for Carl and it was ironical that later in the war he was to move to the *Daily Express*, Fleet

Street's most prominent and successful right-wing newspaper through whose pages 'he was to entertain the nation for half a century.

Carl's politics, when closely considered, are not to be taken too seriously. He simply wanted to draw for the world and what better place than in a publication

46

whose circulation was one of the largest in the country? It was his stage. Indeed, he described the *Daily Express* as his 'Palladium'.

Both on the *Express* and *Reynolds*, Carl was deeply involved with the war. Not all the funnier aspects of the conflict found their way into print.

'I remember once while I was with *Reynolds*,' he recalls with great merriment, 'when, because of a raid which had affected our own office, we were over at the *Sketch*. We had a reciprocal arrangement, you see.

'A lot of journalists were in the Home Guard and came to work in their uniforms and had their rifles propped against the wall. They would even go off to the pub at lunchtime with them. You can imagine the scene in the office: a long room with lines of desks; the editor's office at the end and all these newspaper chaps with uniforms and guns.

'One early morning an officer came in and one of the blokes stood up, snapped his heels together and banged his machine gun on the floor. Well, he had left the safety catch off and – ba-ba-ba-bam – he put six right through the ceiling. You should have seen people move. I was under the table as quick as any of 'em.'

Carl enjoys the memory.

'Didn't you draw a cartoon of it?'

'No, no, you didn't think of it at the time. You were looking for things to draw, but not things involving yourself.'

Equally and more understandably, he found nothing to draw following the night of 16 April 1941.

Carl was working at his desk well into the spring evening as the first wave of German bombers picked out the great S-bend in the Thames east of the City, and began their run, via the docks, over the centre of London. Five hundred aircraft were to drop 100,000 bombs on London that night, one of the worst bombing raids of the war. The fires of the incendiaries spread a glow about the capital, a glow which appeared from above to be coming from within the earth itself, illuminating the dome of St Paul's Cathedral and the

huge vaulting roofs, further west, of the railway stations.

Near King's Cross station, the bespectacled Carl, utterly preoccupied as ever with his work and refusing, like his colleagues, to take any form of cover, bent over his sketch. A few hundred yards away down Great Percy Street, Joan Clarke, Carl's fiancée, was trying to

'What d'you mean: ONLY one of his nuisance raids!!'

The early air raids by the Germans were known as 'nuisance' raids. This was an early Giles cartoon in Reynolds News.

'If they keep on bombing Germany, their railways will soon be as bad as ours, won't they, sir?'

Sunday Express, Feb. 4th, 1945

Giles has suffered a long grievance with British railways. In the war delays and other hiccups to the service were perhaps more understandable. Note the timetable on the station wall.

sleep on the ground floor of the house. In the basement flat, sheltering under a table, were Joan's mother, Agnes, and three of her aunts. The bombs were shaking the foundations.

Agnes eventually called up the stairs and persuaded Joan to come down and take proper refuge. The women drew close. So did the bombs.

Crump, crump, CRASH. CRASH. CRASH. One by one the bombs marched up Great Percy Street. Two of them straddled the Clarke home, one in the road, one in the back garden. One hit the building. The house was demolished. Masonry, timber and tons of bricks avalanched into the basement. The five terrified women were covered in dust but otherwise unharmed. They saw that the blast had blown open the door of the room, a stroke of luck which, they were soon to discover, saved their lives.

Joan, still in her dressing gown and slippers, led her mother and aunts to the door and they all scrambled up via a gap in the rubble through the smoking ruins out onto what a few moments before had been Great Percy Street.

Joan recalls: 'There really wasn't a street there any more. The sky was lit up with all the fires and the bombs were still falling. It was just like you've seen in all those photographs. We were aware of what sounded like heavy rain, but it was a great torrent of rushing water. The mains had been ruptured. We didn't realise it at the time but the people opposite, whose house also had been hit, were being drowned. As were other neighbours. Their basement doors had stayed shut, unlike ours, and had been blocked by the falling timbers and bricks.

'They had presumably survived the actual explosions, like us, but were trapped. They couldn't get out and where they were just filled up with water.'

At *Reynolds News*, Carl realised that this was a particularly bad night and that bombs had fallen over an area which included Great Percy Street.

'The thing was you usually got used to it,' he says. 'I mean it happened every night and you could set your watch by them. You would say: "They're ten minutes late tonight." But that particular time it was bloody terrifying. Eventually I left the office and made my way slowly to Joan's house, ducking and diving in doorways.'

Joan, her mother and aunts were bundled away from immediate danger by air raid wardens and found their way into a relatively undamaged area. The small group of trembling, deeply shocked women walked down Amwell Street into Lloyd Square and stopped outside the familiar and reassuring door of the local convent.

They knocked. The large door was opened by the old caretaker, someone Joan knew, who invited the shivering and grateful group inside. There was a swish of robes and an imposing nun swept down the stairs.

'Who are these people?' she asked. The caretaker muttered the beginning of an explanation.

'Well, they can't stay here,' said the woman of God. And thus the family were ushered cruelly back onto the street. They eventually found refuge at the house of a relative.

In the morning the ladies returned to Great Percy Street to survey the wreck of their home and investigate the possibility of rescuing a few belongings. Joan was thinking of Carl. He, too, might have been bombed. He might have been killed. She borrowed some coins to telephone him, but the lines were down.

In the event, 'We sort of bumped into one another,' says Carl. 'Almost by accident. There she was in the street looking awful. I'd seen the remains of the house and thought they must all have been killed. There was no one you could ask, they were all too busy lookin' after themselves.

'Joan wasn't hurt, as it turned out, but the doctor said she was suffering from nervous disability. But then that covered anything in those days. Her nails went black, I remember.'

Carl is also quick to recall the comical moments of that morning as they tried to recover some of their belongings from the rubble.

'I was looking into a hole in the pile of bricks and thinking of going in,' he says. 'And suddenly I saw this little figure coming out. It was Joan's mother, Agnes. She was a very little woman. She was a jockey's daughter.

'They had hoarded lots of tins and they were all down there in the water. So the labels had all come off. You can imagine, all those tins and not knowing what was in them. You had tomato soup when you wanted tinned peaches. For months.'

At the end of September 1944 the Allies mounted a bold airborne operation which was designed to shorten the war by several months. It ended in bloody failure. It was to become known by the name of the Dutch town at the centre of the attack, Arnhem.

General Eisenhower's plan was that his First Airborne Army would seize three bridges, giving the Allies control of the lower Rhine. The US airborne division was to seize those at Nijmegen and Grave, while the First British Airborne Division was ordered to capture the furthest bridge over the Rhine at Arnhem.

The British Guards Armoured Division would force their way through the German lines to relieve the airborne forces.

The operation was a catastrophe. The Germans put

Giles sits on a wrecked German gun in Holland in 1945.

up a formidable opposition. The battle was fierce and cruel and after eight days the British pulled back across the Rhine. Of the original 10,000 troops, 2,400 returned.

Observing it all, with a tin helmet, sketch pad and a clutch of sharpened pencils, was a young cartoonist who had been sent over by his boss Arthur Christiansen, the legendary editor of the *Daily Express*. He perched wherever he could, attempting to avoid the rush and dash of those involved in more important matters, and drew cartoons in his capacity as an official Fleet Street war correspondent. His rank was captain. Captain Giles, indeed. If only Chalkie could have seen him.

Carl was conscious that his contribution to the operation might not be fully appreciated by those at the sharp end. He returned more than once to the theme that what soldiers needed from England was certainly not a bloke from Fleet Street with a pencil and a drawing pad.

One cartoon showed him arriving at a forward artillery unit. The benumbed twenty-five-pounder battery look him over and one of the crew remarks: 'We asked for ammo – and they send us a war correspondent.'

Carl was flown in with other correspondents by Dakota. 'I was at Nijmegen and Eindhoven,' he says. 'We watched the action from the other side. We couldn't cross the river, just saw the shelling. It was a bit noisy for me.'

He was to travel back and forth, between home and the war in Europe, a number of times. He observed the gradual crumbling of German resolve, the routing of its armies and its final defeat as witnessed in Field Marshal Montgomery's tent on the desolate Lüneberg Heath on 4 May 1945. Captain Giles was there, standing on the edge of history, with his pad.

But in his reminiscences it is not the great shuddering moment of history, not the meetings of kings and generals, the clash of warlords that catch Carl's fancy, but the daft encounters in the undergrowth of these mighty affairs. In the slit trenches. In the bog-house.

Carl poses against a Jeep. He loved Jeeps and used to terrorise Suffolk in one.

Carl tells the story of how he and some men in a recce party were half crawling along a trench near the front one day when he saw a group of Coldstream Guards moving in the opposite direction. He peered at the grimy face beneath the tin helmet of the corporal leading the other party and saw startlingly familiar features. It took a moment or two to register, for you do not expect to meet anybody from your high street in a slit trench hundreds of kilometres from nowhere. Suddenly there was recognition. The chap before him was his bank manager from Barclays, Ipswich.

'Here,' said the bank manager. 'I've got your brother-in-law in my lot. Come and say hello.' The two men moved down the trench in search of Carl's relative.

'He was in the shit-house,' recalls Carl. 'There we were all that way from home and he was in the shit-house. We had to stand around outside waiting for him to finish.'

Carl's companions for much of his time in Europe were the famous war correspondent Alan Moorehead of the *Daily Express*, and Chris Buckley of the *Daily Telegraph*. Moorehead's ability to speak fluent German proved useful on more than one occasion.

'We couldn't have done without him,' says Carl. 'In Holland he actually saved us from being captured.

'We were in a Jeep and we came across this other Jeep full of German correspondents. They were all armed to the teeth. Rifles and so on. We had no guns, except the driver who had a rifle.

'Alan went up to these Hitler Youth types and spoke to them. He could even laugh and joke in German.

'We ended up drinking Scotch and sitting about as if we were all in the same army.'

As well as seeing the funnier side of the war, Carl also suffered, as many did, the terrible trauma of being among the first of the Allies to enter a concentration camp. He was with the Coldstream Guards, deep inside

'Be funny if the siren went now, wouldn't it?'

Sunday Express, Aug. 19th, 1945

London celebrates VJ-day (victory – the final victory of the Second World War – over Japan). It would be impossible to count all the festive figures in this cartoon, but each one seems to have been allowed a character of its own. Look at the two figures to the right of the picture, half way up, who have just hurled a bobby into the air.

'Taxi!'

Giles' drawings of GIs became particularly famous during the war. They were loved by both the British and the Americans. The former thought they were rude, the latter regarded them as flattering.

This most celebrated of cartoons pokes fun at the American habit of monopolising the taxis – anywhere. Here, a member of a crashed Flying Fortress crew hails a passing Gestapo staff car in Berlin.

'Rare boys for souvenirs, these Americans.' Sunday Express, July 15th, 1945

Another of Giles' cartoons ribbed the Americans for their souvenir-hunting habits. The round circle of light in the tower above the Palace of Westminster betrays the absence of the world's most famous timepiece.

Germany, when, in May 1945, they approached the perimeter fence of the vast compound which took its name from the beautiful town nearby, Belsen.

It was high summer and the region was sweltering in a heatwave.

This was the weather of his Suffolk childhood. This was the sort of day when Carl, visiting his parents' farming family as he often did as a young boy, had seen the corn stand still and blaze with gold.

This was the heat, too, of Chalkie's classroom. Windows open, equations squeaked onto the blackboard, thoughts far away.

Nothing moved, not a bird, in the hedgerows. This was the glorious weather of the summer harbour, yachts' sails listlessly searching for the lazy wind, girls on decks, shirtless men perspiring as they paddled their dinghies here and there. Dogs yapping at the water's edge.

Halcyon days, they always called them.

Until now.

There was almost nothing that Carl had seen in the whole of his life that could not be cheered up with a stroke of his pen.

Until now.

'I didn't want to go in. I stopped at the gate. The smell was unimaginable,' recalls Carl. 'But a colleague called Paul Holt said: "You must go in. You have to. When you see this in the papers you won't believe it any more than the readers will. But we have to tell what we've seen. We must go in."

'There were mountains of dead bodies – white, terrible – and the guards were still walking around, unbelievably, with whips hanging by straps from their wrists.

'Two trains had just come in and you could hear screaming from the trucks.

'We saw that woman who was known as the Beast of Belsen. And we saw the Kommandant, Kramner. I've still got his armband with a swastika on it.

'Some of the loutish guards were beaten by the British soldiers. The officers turned a blind eye. You wanted to put the boot in yourself, but you didn't. I saw some of the bloody results and they were such a mess, smashed, bleeding faces, they no longer looked like human beings. Some of them, I think, must have been dead. I suppose we were behaving as badly as them, but you didn't think that at the time. And you didn't care, of course.

'After they had taken all the camp guards away they gave the people in there a dance. It was weird. Macabre. We all danced with them, putting heavy arms round them. They were just bones, wearing strips of cloth.

'I was billeted up at a luxurious hunting lodge. We were up there in the bar – I was drinking with a little Aussie correspondent called Ronnie Monson. Also in there was this big fat German, a businessman or something, in hunting jacket and boots. He was laughing with some friends. Ronnie put his drink down and laid into him. He put him down on the floor. Really let him have it. And Ronnie was only a little bugger. This German's nose was bleeding and he was grunting and groaning.

'We all felt so much anger that it is difficult to put it into words.

'Not a day or even a night goes by now when I don't think of Belsen. It was the most dreadful, terrible thing in my life.

'Chris [Arthur Christiansen] asked me, at the time, to do some drawings.

'I refused. What could my drawings say after those nightmare photographs?'

The year before his duties in Europe, Carl and Joan had rented a naval officer's cottage on the outskirts of Ipswich in Suffolk. Carl adored East Anglia and had visited the area, where his mother's family had long been Norfolk farming people, regularly as a child. He had also, until his brother's sudden death, worked for a happy spell in Ipswich.

Now he had, as it were, finally emigrated from

London. He was home. There was to be a change of house. Twice. But Suffolk, with its hardy, decent people, its estuary taverns and its chilly sailing waters, was where he would stay.

During that period of the war, Carl's social and home life was dominated by his friendship with GIs. He loved Americans and, in particular, the American military. His wartime cartoons were celebrated for their depiction of cigar-chomping, grinning Yankee servicemen.

One of the most celebrated sketches, which appeared in the *Sunday Express* on 23 April 1944 during the apprehensive months before D-Day, concerned the Americans' infuriating talent for monopolising taxis. The old wartime cliché was that Yanks were 'over-paid, over-sexed and over here'. But nothing caused more bitter resentment of their high-profile presence than the fact that whenever a British chap waved his brolly at a London taxi it would whizz past full of lantern-jawed, Lucky Strike-smoking American servicemen – often with pretty English girls, expensive perfume wafting from the windows, giggling on their laps.

Says Carl: 'The British used to think that I was being unkind. But, you know, the Americans loved them. They are a cartoon people. They understood them and appreciated them.'

Carl enjoyed the GIs' uncomplicated good humour, their brash though engaging masculinity, their generosity of spirit, their laughter, their style and their uniforms. East Anglia, with its numerous airfields, swarmed with them. Many drank ale in the Fountain, Carl's local pub in the attractive village of Tuddenham.

It was there that he befriended a group of black GIs who were building runways at a local airbase. A close friendship grew and soon his new pals were using the Giles house as a home from home. They slept there and ate there. The cosy East Anglian cottage rang nightly with a joyful blend of far-flung interests and cultures; the Deep South and Suffolk ale, Harlem and home-cooked English puddings, Dixie and the *Daily Express*, Lord Beaverbrook and Louis Armstrong, childhood in the ghettos and Chalkie.

Joan somehow managed to keep the fit frames of these splendid grandsons of sons of sons of cotton slaves well fuelled with home-concocted 'chow', despite the miseries of rationing.

'The house was full of endless laughter,' recalls Carl. 'Yes, the villagers were astonished to see these black American servicemen. They'd not seen their like before. But they took to them too. Some of the local girls even found themselves in the family way.'

The most memorable aspect of the association, one that is recalled with pleasure by older taverners of those parts, was the raggletaggle jazz band which Carl formed with his rhythmic and musical chums in the public bar of the Fountain.

Carl's friendship with the Yanks of East Anglia, black and white, became famous back home in the States. An American correspondent of the time wrote: 'Giles was one of the new English humorists to seize upon the rich subject of the three million Yanks who invaded Britain during the war. A great fan of the United States, he loved American bombast and gadgetry.

OPPOSITE: *In the photograph we reproduce here the characters in the Fountain include two of Carl's GI friends, Butch playing the drums and John Louis facing the camera. Standing to the right of Carl in Naval uniform is local lad, Eric Ossard, known always as 'Dotsie'. Dotsie at the time was serving in the Navy and is seen here at home on leave. His ship was the*

Shearwater, *a corvette protecting packets plying between Southend and Antwerp. Carl had given him a lift in his car when he had spotted him walking to Ipswich station. He was, that very day, off to join the Navy. They have been friends ever since and Dotsie, for many years now, has been Carl's chum about the farm and tireless odd-job man.*

'I don't care if the war is nearly over—I'm not selling my cab for a fiver for a souvenir.'

This cartoon combines the two principal American 'sins' of taxi-hogging and memento-grabbing. London cabbies, it suggests, are not to be bought. Not for a wretched fiver, anyway.

'So!! Watch the Boat Race without paying entertainment tax would he? Take him away, men!'

Sunday Express, March 31st, 1946

One of the disagreeable manifestations of post-war austerity was the levying of an entertainment tax. The cartoon shows Giles' life-long dislike of petty officialdom.

'Well I'm dashed! We were right that time—goody goody!'   *Daily Express, Feb. 28th, 1946*

With the war well and truly over the British could return happily to whingeing about the weather. Giles often declares a passionate contempt for weather forecasters. See how the joy of the met men contrasts with the appalling misery of Londoners in the cold. Note the sundial, a redundant object, tucked away in the Air Ministry porch. This cartoon is an early example of Giles' superb use of snow.

'I'm on a bike—what are you on?'　　　　　　　　　**Daily Express, Sept. 10th, 1946**

Heavy flooding in the South of England. Such acts of God are no respecters of class.

'He roared at the staggering variety of US Army clothing but learned to draw the garments down to the last seam. He loved our drooping socks, sloppy field jackets and chevrons – which seemed to the English to have as many rungs as a fireman's ladder.

'When the first Americans moved into his neighbourhood near the lovely village of Tuddenham, Giles became their friend and local champion. The soldiers were members of an engineering battalion who were bulldozing, grading and levelling concrete 24 hours a day to get the Ninth Airforce's Marauders into the air. On Saturday evenings the negro engineers would cycle into the local pub, the Fountain, balancing bass fiddles, drums, trumpets, trombones and saxophones and other instruments on their handlebars.

'The bass player would angle his instrument at sixty degrees in order to clear the low ceiling with its Scotch thistles, Tudor roses and fleurs-de-lis impressed there by Elizabethan workmen.

'The Suffolk farmers would then crowd into the back

'We three kings of Orient are...'

Sunday Express, Dec. 21st, 1947

Two years into peace. But no peace in this picture. Here are three of Giles' monster children united by youthful greed and malevolence. All they want is for the owner of the house to put a sixpence in their grubby little hands so they can move on to torment the unsuspecting people next door.

room with their pints of mild and bitter as Giles struck up the opening bars on the piano and the sixteen-piece hot band went into "Fat Mama With The Meat Shakin' On Her Bones".'

The joy of jazz in the Fountain was to be fairly short-lived. Carl's friends from the base were soon moved on and contact was lost.

'They specially got on with me,' says Carl. 'They

'I'll bet he's ever so miserable on Sundays—not able to keep slamming these in people's faces.'

Daily Express, June 7th, 1949

Giles hated level crossings and their keepers. He was driving back to his Suffolk home one night to find himself barred by a gate across the line. He would have had to detour for miles. The keeper had gone to bed. Giles shouted his

indignation until the lights went on and the chap stuck his head out of the window. There was a long and fierce argument until the man finally came down and let Giles through. Giles loathed anything that impeded his motoring.

knew, you see, their colour didn't matter a damn. They could have been black, green or blue as far as I was concerned.'

Certainly the integrated harmonies of the Fountain were in rugged contrast to the other pubs of the area.

Cockney writer Johnny Speight, creator of television's ranting working-class bigot Alf Garnett, and one of Carl's closest friends, was himself based in the area during the war. He didn't know Carl at the time but he tells a story which is certainly relevant to events at Tuddenham.

'I was in this Suffolk pub one evening – I forget which it was – and there were all these Americans in there creating a bloody riot. They were objecting to the fact that one of their black soldiers had taken up with a local girl. A white girl, of course. They had 'im up at one end of the bar and they were goin' to lynch 'im. It was bloody terrifying.

'Then this village copper comes in – a real country bobby – and elbows his way through. It was almost as if he had said, "'Ello, 'ello, 'ello." He hadn't even got a truncheon with him. Well, they all fell back and it went quiet. They had been confronted by the full majesty of the law. It was amazing. He just led the bloke out. And that was before all the American military police could get there with all their riot sticks and heavy gear.'

Things were to change at the Fountain too. When the black soldiers had gone, a number of white GIs took their place.

Carl had done paintings of his friends – one of them is reproduced in the colour section – and they had been hung up in the bar. When it became clear that these pictures were going to cause offence to the white Americans, the woman who ran the establishment quickly took them down.

'It was a bloody disgrace,' says Carl.

Giles originals don't usually find themselves treated with such contempt – though there is the story of another Giles cartoon which says more for the artist than it does for the London publican who possesses it.

Carl, who was seldom known to visit only one hostelry per drinking excursion, had dropped into an establishment which he hadn't been to before, accompanied by his friend Johnny Speight. He was surprised to see an original on the wall.

'I wonder where he got that,' he whispered to Speight. 'Excuse me,' he said to the proprietor with feigned uncertainty. 'Isn't that a Giles original?'

'It is, sir.'

'Where did you get it?'

'From the artist.'

'Do you know him?' enquired Carl lightly.

'Know him? Know him?' said the publican, polishing a glass and holding it to the light. 'Yeah, I know him. Wish I didn't sometimes.'

'What's he like?' asked Carl.

'Well, he's like all artists – he's talented, you know – but he drinks too much. I've had to throw him out of here several times. In fact I'll tell you now that Giles gave me that cartoon because...' and here the tavern host looked about him as if searching for the trembling earlobes of indiscreet eavesdroppers '...because he couldn't pay the bill.'

Speight and Carl withdrew with their drinks. 'Why didn't you tell him who you were?' asked Speight.

'Why humiliate the man?' said Carl.

Explains Speight: 'Carl was amused. He enjoyed it. What you've got to understand about him is that he is fascinated by what motivates people. He collects characters. Apart from the booze and the socialising, that's why he likes pubs so much. Life for Carl is a stage for comedy.'

"Right — on the show of hands the turkey gets a reprieve — one of you go to the shop and get six large tins of corn beef."

This was also in aid of the Royal National Institute for the Deaf. Carl himself is almost entirely deaf in one ear, the result of a motorcycle accident in 1935.

Every year Giles drew Daily Express *Christmas cards for charity. This inevitably snowy illustration of a not-so-Silent Night was done for the Royal National Institute for the Deaf in 1982.*

This was drawn in aid of the Game Conservancy Research Fund. Giles' cartoons for this charity were auctioned at the Game Conservancy May Ball and also used as Christmas cards. Note the fox fur round Grandma's neck. When such things began to upset animal lovers, the fur disappeared.

Giles' favourite charity was the Royal National Lifeboat Institution. His efforts, through auctioned originals and Christmas cards, raised millions of pounds. However, to anyone who has a dark fear of cracking ice this drawing may seem rather less then festive.

Another masterful painting for the R.N.L.I.

This is another popular Christmas card.

Giles' snow effects are quite outstanding in colour. In this Christmas card, it is the parking meter attendant who is the subject of seasonal goodwill.

The particularly splendid detail in this card for Game Conservancy is the trail of fox-prints up against the wall on the right. It can be seen just how stealthily the beast approached the open boot of the car.

Outside the back door in this card the freshly fallen snow lies an inch thick on the dustbin-lid.
Christmases in Gilesland were, simply, always white.

"Wait till they get to the bit about 'Peace on Earth' then let 'em have it"

Another Christmas card. For once the carollers, so often villainous to behold, have a saintly look.

This is Ike, the 6ft 6in GI, stationed in Suffolk, who became such a close friend of Carl's and Joan's. He often stayed with the couple, along with his friends – 'Tex' and others – and he played the double bass in the small noisy band which Giles formed at his local pub, the Fountain.

Giles did twelve paintings for the 1978 Guinness calendar. Here, the Giles front parlour, where a young suitor is proposing to Carol, has become very Guinnessy. Note Grandma playing the harp in the picture by the door.

Any sailor who studies this Guinness calendar picture for August will be horrified by the state of the British group's boat.

This picture marked September for the Guinness calendar. King Tut appears to have swigged the explorer's drink. Note the instruction on the end of the sarcophagus.

In this Guinness calendar picture for December, Grandma enjoys a 3am noggin with Santa. Note Grandma, on the wall, in her schooldays.

CHAPTER FOUR

Fleet Street and 'The Family'

Carl Giles despises publicity. He loathes being interviewed. Indeed, he has never allowed himself to be interrogated on the radio or on television and regards any attempt to lure him towards a microphone or a camera lens as a monstrous impertinence. The *This Is Your Life* show, a half-hour television programme which surprises its victim in the street and submits him or her to a reunion with a lifetime of friends and relations and schoolmates, has often attempted to set up one of these traps for Carl. Once he caught his mother secretively poking around in old boxes, digging up documents pertaining to his life. It was clear she had been 'approached'.

Says Carl with a mixture of affection and extreme irritation: 'She'd let anyone in. If the Germans had come over here and kicked down her door, she'd have made them a cup of tea and bought a copy of *Mein Kampf* off them.'

Such an extreme piece of imagery, as posthumous retribution towards his much-loved mum, illustrates Carl's intense dislike of any form of invasion. In Ipswich a double-glazing man telephoned as we were having supper. Joan answered the call.

'Who was that?' asked Carl, with lurking suspicion.

'A double-glazing man,' replied Joan, returning to the table and anticipating the response.

'Good God,' grumped Carl furiously, throwing

Grandma as Britannia. The detail is splendid in this picture; the white fox fur keeps her neck snug, her handbag is secure with a padlock and ready to strike at all invaders and her brolly, held proud, could command the very clouds to unfold. Those who know her creator may find the expression on her face somewhat familiar. Could she be Giles? Butch lies, as vigilant as he is able, at her feet.

'Same old thing every Sunday after the Boat Race—"Please, Mr. Evans, can you get my boy's 'ead out of your fence?"'

Sunday Express, March 29th, 1953

In Giles' world the principal aggravation in life, for the police as for just about anyone else, was the existence of little boys.

down his napkin and making a token but surprisingly vigorous attempt to rise from his wheelchair. 'God. The bastards, the buggers. Bloody infernal...' Carl continued to mutter and grunt for a moment. Then he got over it and smiled. 'I love to get at them,' he said with passion. 'God, how I love to get at them.'

He was fond of the late Jean Rook of the *Daily Express* and demonstrated his affection by poking fun at her in his cartoons. However, even Jean received a fairly discouraging lack of enthusiasm from him when she attempted to interview him for their own newspaper.

Wrote Jean: 'When I asked The Master for lunch, he forgot the date twice and turned up once at the wrong restaurant.'

Fleet Street's celebrated lady inquisitor, Lynn Barber, had similar difficulties. She wrote: 'My day started badly on Ipswich station when he said he really wasn't

'We're playing safe this week—we're sending Sidney across the road in a barrel.'

Sunday Express, Oct. 18th, 1953

Here again, in a cartoon marking 1953's National Safety Week, the kids have devised their own ingenious way, under the disapproving nose of the law, of celebrating the occasion. The town bobby is too appalled by the sight of the barrel containing Sidney to notice what is going on behind the tree.

'If I'd painted it on a horse and signed it "Munnings" they'd have accepted it.'

Daily Express, April 30th, 1954

Giles pokes fun here at modern art. He enjoyed, at the time, a close friendship with the late Alfred Munnings, the masterful painter of horses. Munnings lived in Suffolk and employed in service Giles' Aunt May and her husband, a former sergeant major in the Royal Artillery. In the sketch, standing by the door, is a pensive-looking George, the intellectual of the Giles Family, always known as the bookworm.

'I should take your little joke off the wall— here comes your Missus.'

Daily Express, Dec. 24th, 1956

Giles was fascinated by nurses, though he has been known to rail at them. Note the figures in the right-hand corner. As so often in a Giles drawing you are taken beyond the frame of the picture.

meeting me at all – he'd changed the appointment.' Lynn did manage to conduct some kind of an interview, in time, but complained gently that she had only managed to extract an even mildly useful nugget of information every half-hour or so.

Her problem was that Carl, quite happy to discuss the virtues of other artists, was disinclined to talk about himself. Wrote Lynn, in the *Sunday Express* colour magazine: 'But come on, Giles, what of Giles?

This isn't supposed to be a seminar on twentieth-century cartoonists; it's an interview. "Grk," he goes. "Humph." Whenever you ask him any questions about himself, he suddenly turns deaf and grumbles like a wounded seagull, "grk, grk..." When I asked which of his cartoons he most liked he grked like a whole flock of seagulls and insisted that I have some pudding.

'Later, on the way out to his farm, I was rash

69

'Please can we have our ball?'

Daily Express, June 5th, 1958

The old buffer in the foreground is so horrified by what has occurred that he simply hasn't moved a muscle.
He is stunned.

enough to praise Grandma while we were stuck at a roundabout – he put the Range Rover into reverse and hurtled backwards towards a line of traffic. I learned not to ask questions about Giles while he was driving.'

There is one television film, made in good faith and with Carl's grudging approval, which is intended to be a profile, one of those half-hour biographical documentary tributes. In this particular effort, simply titled *Giles*, all manner of those who have been associated with Carl are presented as talking heads. The heads don't actually deliver very much information, merely tell us what a splendid person Carl was, and is, how he liked a drink and what quite wonderful cartoons he drew.

At one point in the film the camera, in close-up, shows Carl at work in his studio, half leaning in characteristic fashion over his drawing. It has evidently intruded. For he looks up, very irritated, and gives one of his 'grk' noises.

To say that Carl is a private person would be silly. There is nothing private about the way in which he has enjoyed himself, in taverns or wherever else, and he is not coy or bashful, secretive or timid. He simply doesn't want people prodding and poking about in his life who

Mother's Day. Give her a rest from cooking—take her out for a picnic.

Sunday Express, March 27th, 1960

A spring outing for Giles' most celebrated creation, the Family. A bee attempts to take pollen from the flowers on

Grandma's hat. The padlock has not yet appeared on her handbag.

71

'Just listen to all those "Cors!" and "Oos!" and long low whistles.'

Sunday Express, Oct. 23rd, 1960

D.H. Lawrence's Lady Chatterley's Lover, *written in 1928 and described as a gospel of sexual fulfilment, received extravagant publicity when it became the subject of a pornography trial in 1960. The judge instructed the jury to go away and read it. Penguin, the publishers, won the case and sold their entire run of 200,000 copies on the day of publication. Giles had a good feel for the stonework of court buildings.*

haven't been invited; doesn't want intimacy of any kind from those who don't qualify; doesn't wish to speak of his work, which he feels should speak for itself, with those who may be too daft and insensitive to see what he's on about. There is a strong element of 'them and us' in all of this. The 'them', for example, include those with whom he has had to deal, all of his professional life, who cannot understand why he should need an extra half-hour to complete a sketch – bugger the edition times – or those who believe that no harm can

'Just leave it there one minute over time, my lad—that's all.'

Daily Express, Feb. 7th, 1961

Solicitors had accused police of being over zealous. Note the terrible old rascal of a legal figure getting into his Rolls.

be done by trimming a bit off a Giles cartoon in order, in those most dreaded of words, to 'make it fit'.

There was a production man on the *Daily Express* whom Carl nicknamed, with deep feeling, 'Slasher'. For Slasher would actually cut half an inch of 'expendable' sky off the top of a Giles picture. Carl would be reduced to a terrible state of rage, agitation and, above all, frustration. For Slasher couldn't understand the importance of that strip of sky. To Carl, this was barbarism. Slasher's attitude was intolerable. Slasher was one of 'them'.

'Stop fretting, Vera—powerboats have to give way to sail.'   *Daily Express, Sept. 6th, 1962*

Anyone who has sailed in busy water, as Giles has, will understand the fragile nature of this 'rule of the road'.

Grandma and her crew appear not to have a life-jacket between them.

74

Carl's friend, writer and comedian Eric Sykes, says: 'Carl doesn't want to have to explain himself. On any level. Not just about work. About everything. To be a friend of Carl is to be a member of an unofficial club where everyone has an unseen secret sign. What it means is that everyone understands one another. Like brothers talking about the same father.

'Carl loves that. He simply doesn't want to explain or justify. Of course he can be crotchety. Who can blame him? Anyway, he's an artist. He's creative. He doesn't want some idiot asking him about Grandma. Grandma's there, for goodness sake.'

So Carl, as his fame grew, was to discourage the professional curiosity of fellow newspapermen. Apart from those awkward recent attempts at an encounter by Jean Rook and Lynn Barber, there is little evidence of any journalist persuading him to say anything on the record whatsoever. Except 'grk'.

Of journalistic drinking chums, there was never a shortage. Carl, who worked from his studio in Ipswich and sent his cartoons to London by train (hereby a later tale), would descend on the metropolis every ten days or so with the express and determined purpose of having an extremely good time in selected drinking establishments of the parish.

These were numerous.

Few pubs and wine bars were more permanently and generously patronised than those of the old Fleet Street, the historic thoroughfare – boulevard of broken dreams, it was more absurdly called by some romantic drunk – which leads from the bottom of the Strand down towards the noble and often blurred magnificence of St Paul's, standing proud and disapproving at the gate of the City.

There was, and is, the Albion on Ludgate Circus, at the corner of Fleet Street, and a few yards further along on the left towards the Strand, the Punch.

The former, a favourite of printers, always seemed to smell horribly of sizzling meat on a Sunday lunchtime and the latter was – it must all be in the past tense, alas, for none of us go to these places now – a large noisy, smoky place with ancient *Punch* cartoons, in frames, all over the wall. Then, further up Fleet Street opposite the great black glass-fronted façade of the *Daily Express*, there was the Eight Bells. This tavern, as yellow and smoky as the rest of them, nestled in the spiritual shadow of St Bride's, Fleet Street's own church.

Carl knew all the pubs, of course, but his two favourites were Poppins, an extraordinary little one-horse saloon tucked into the side of the *Daily Express* in Poppins Court (on the right side, looking up Fleet Street) and the famous El Vino, up on the left and nearly opposite the law courts. The original Poppins, or Pops – it was actually called the Red Lion – has long gone now but I remember it as a most seedy little place, decorated with the requisite nicotine patina and narrow like a train corridor.

It was a Hogarthian dump, where the famous became inebriated with the infamous, where great headlines popped like genies out of tumblers and where at least one famous political commentator used to sleep on the floor among the fag ends and the large important shoes of those who imbibed and roared with merriment above him.

Giles loved Poppins and could usually be found there on his trips to the office from the country, forays which often caused havoc of some kind or another. His editor, Arthur Christiansen, wrote affectionately of Carl in his autobiography, *Headlines All My Life*. He had been listing, at some length, the various frustrations suffered by the editor of the *Daily Express*, especially those created by professionally discomfited important members of the staff.

'Here is Giles, the great Giles, in eruption on the telephone,' recalled 'Chris', as he was universally known. 'He is the apple of Lord Beaverbrook's eye since the proprietor spotted him drawing for *Reynolds*, the Co-op Sunday paper, and persuaded John Gordon to sign him up for the *Sunday Express* at twenty

'Another lettuce-leaf lunch like this and the Express'll be getting a series from me on "How I killed my wife".'

Daily Express, March 20th, 1962

A doctor had warned that over-eating kills. Salads, he suggested, were the thing to keep you healthy. Here, a group of Giles' British workmen eat their 'dinner' while considering the matter. The notion that such a man should be required to nibble lettuce for his health while toiling in such tough and hazardous circumstances, perched on a girder, adds a further comic element to this idea.

guineas a week. "What's the matter with you, Carl? Want to come up to London to discuss things? All right, but don't be late – I'm busy."

'Giles is not late, but by the time I am ready to take him for lunch, he has disappeared.

'He has gone to Poppins to buy drinks for Anne Edwards, Eve Perrick and Drusilla Beyfus. When I catch up with him he is in high good humour; the girls make a great fuss of him and he is snorting incoherently to express his pleasure.

'I look at this curious wisp of a man with affectionate curiosity. Unlike Osbert Lancaster, a product of the Slade School, Carl Giles has never had an art lesson in his life.'

The only formal training Carl ever had, in fact, was from anatomy classes at night school.

'He lives on a farm outside Ipswich where he has built his own studio, brick by brick, plank by plank. Hobbies: making furniture, building caravans, selling cattle, riding point-to-point, welding, knocking down walls, rebuilding them, making aquariums, drinking, playing the piano (jazz or classical), home movies, entertaining GIs based in East Anglia, boating, fast cars, dogs. All these things he does with as much gusto as he draws his cartoons – and he loves cartooning so much that he once drew 137 separate characters in just one of them.

'My arrival at Poppins does not dampen anyone's spirits, and I have the utmost difficulty in getting him to leave the place. The girls go reluctantly, and other customers buttonhole Giles and buy him "just a small one for the road". "Now you see why I hate coming to London," he grins into his glass.'

Later that day the mighty Lord Beaverbrook was to call down to Christiansen and say: 'I hear Giles is in town. Send him along to see me.'

Once again, Carl had disappeared. Christiansen, realising that the pubs were closed, ordered a runner of some kind to try the press club. Not there! In that case, ordered the editor, London must be searched, every Ipswich-bound train apprehended before its departure from Liverpool Street. It was, of course, always the way when a newspaperman was required by the proprietor and was not to be found in any of the more obvious localities. Every off-limits drinking hole, be it a room at the top of rickety Soho stairs or hellish basement den, has often been called by a desperate junior executive in the search for reporter, photographer or, indeed, cartoonist. The panic on this occasion was unnecessary, for Carl was found in the photo-engraving department arguing with the overseer about the making of line blocks.

Recalled Christiansen: 'He reappeared in my room like a genie-out-of-a-bottle and I am so happy he is found again that I forgive all the chaos he had caused me...

'Two days later, a souvenir to commemorate this day is delivered. It is a full-size cartoon for my private collection, and it shows me sitting at my desk, my brow furrowed, my aspect grim. Around the door a tiny, shrinking nervous figure which does not reach up to the doorknob gazes at me apprehensively. This is Giles as he sees himself and he is saying: "Tell me, Mr Christiansen, why are you not always cheerful?"'

Such was Carl's status and value that he could treat his employers very much as he wished. Says Bob Edwards, former deputy chairman, Mirror Group Newspapers, who was twice editor of the *Daily Express* (1961, 1963-65): 'Editors treated Giles as a genius. Certainly, there was not one of them who thought of himself as grander than Giles. To risk losing Giles was unthinkable. It would have been a catastrophe.'

Thus it was that Carl was singularly honoured in all manner of ways. He would, unlike fellow cartoonists, simply draw one sketch. Others, like the *Express*'s political propagandist Michael Cummings or the great pocket cartoonist Sir Osbert Lancaster, would nervously approach the editor's office with a number of rough ideas and hope that at least one might meet with approval – or even, possibly, a generous guffaw of appreciative laughter. Sir Osbert, recalls Edwards, was so timid in this regard that he used to stand about outside as, within, the editor may have been discussing international spying scoops with Chapman Pincher. Osbert would eventually press his bewhiskered features against the frosted glass so that he could be identified and so that it could be seen that he awaited an audience.

Carl would draw his cartoon in the privacy of his Ipswich studio, without prior discussion as to the subject matter, and then despatch it to London at the last minute, always with the reluctance of the perfectionist who regards his work as only ever half completed. In the early days it was sent by train but in later years, when this method proved too unreliable, by taxi. It would usually arrive beyond the deadline, a time zone in newspapers which is akin to some terrible betwixt and between hour in Hades.

The fact that this carry-on was permitted for half a century is a measure of the astonishing regard in which Carl was held.

Edwards remembers, as does every other editor of the *Daily* and *Sunday Express*, the appalling tension which built up in the production area of the newspapers as, time after time, the 'Giles' was nowhere to be seen. The minute hands of the many clocks in the newsroom jerked mercilessly round the dial. A vast green plank, ordered there by Beaverbrook himself and suspended from the ceiling amidst the strip lighting, commanded in huge white letters to the toiling shirt-sleeved employees 'MAKE IT ON TIME'.

'When the Giles eventually arrived,' says Edwards, 'we would have to put it into the first editions in halftones, because it was a quicker process.'

Lord Cudlipp, the celebrated former chairman of Mirror Group Newspapers who as plain Mr Hugh Cudlipp was, in those earlier days, managing editor of the *Sunday Express*, also remembers the tension: 'It would be a Saturday night and there would be this huge blank space on page three waiting for the Giles. Carl would have called and told us it was on the 2.10 from Ipswich. At four or five o'clock it still won't have arrived.

'Carl would have said: "Send a messenger. The guard's got it. He's a friend of mine." The cartoon somehow always made it – no one knew quite how.'

Carl wasn't ever easy to deal with. As far as the drama of his cartoon arrival was concerned, those whose professional lives depended on its actually getting into the paper had simply to hang on in there and keep their nerve. There is no doubt that he made editors very agitated indeed.

'I recall him standing there,' says Bob Edwards, remembering the occasions when Carl would actually visit him in his office. 'He would have his head on one side and could be rather irascible.'

Another cause for executives to be uneasy about Carl was the fact that he would sometimes hide in his drawings the odd shocking or rude detail. A nursery scene, for example, might have in some obscure corner the *Daily Express*'s children's favourite, Rupert Bear, hanging from a gibbet.

But more seriously and more alarmingly for editors, certainly during the earlier years, was Carl's favourite sport of adding to any scenes showing American GIs the small and scarcely noticeable detail of a packet of French letters. Condoms, in those days, far from being a common source of conversation in kindergarten as they are now, were simply not spoken of, except by servicemen. For a family newspaper to show pictures of French letter packets tumbling from the pockets of anyone at all would simply have been regarded as disgraceful. Still, a number of Carl's little packets, looking like tiny square envelopes, did manage to get past the trembling magnifying glass of night editors and lawyers. Readers might care to study the cartoon on page 80. A magnifying glass might well be required for those not of ferociously good sight but there are, quite clearly when spotted, two French letter packets in the drawing.

The Royal Commission on the Police reports that there is unsufficient readiness on the part of the public to help the police.
Sunday Express, June 3rd, 1962

Kids versus the law again. Giles' 'twins' can be seen at the end of the line.

'Just like it said in the invite, Tex—"Widow and five single daughters would like to entertain party of American soldiers for Christmas".'

Giles would torment his various editors by tucking rude things away in his drawings. Rupert Bear, loved by all Express readers, would occasionally be found hanging from a gibbet in the corner of a nursery. In his GI pictures the artist would place the odd French letter packet – a tiny square envelope – somewhere in the drawing. Often they had appeared to fall from a GI's pocket. There are two such packets in this wartime picture which escaped the editor's vigilance. It takes some searching; but they are clear enough.

'Dad! Mum says come back and scratch out what you wrote in the Visitors' Book at once.'

Sunday Express, Aug. 12th, 1962

A study of an extremely unhappy Family. A seagull has taken objection to the cloth bird on Grandma's hat.

Says Carl of the then legal manager, Andrew Edwards, whose apparent job it was to supervise good taste as well as legal safety: 'I used to love keeping him in a state.'

Carl could be appalling to cope with when crotchety and out of sorts but, for the most part, he dealt with high newspaper authority with mischievous good humour. Christiansen once admonished Carl in a telegram as being: 'Brilliant, but unpunctual, unreliable and unbusinesslike.'

81

It was the accusation of unpunctuality which, while justified, particularly irritated Carl, for Christiansen was notorious for keeping people waiting. Carl replied with the short missive:

Dear Pot
Thank you for your telegram
                              Kettle.

'The Russians have been round the world twice since Grandma's been in there.'

Daily Express, Aug. 14th, 1962

Two Russian cosmonauts, in orbit around the world in separate craft, were breaking all records for length of time in space.

After one abortive lunch arrangement between Christiansen and Carl, in which the artist had been kept waiting for over an hour, 'Chris' was to receive another cartoon offering which showed two panels of a scene outside his office. The first panel featured a self-portrait of the bespectacled Carl sitting patiently in his overcoat outside the frosted glass of a door on which was the word EDITOR. In the second panel Carl was still there in specs and coat, identically positioned, but the figure had now become a skeleton.

For most of the time Carl's communication with those of any significance who challenged him, irritated him, amused him or impressed him was in the form of cartoon. Marie Stopes, the internationally best-selling author of birth-control matters, shared with Winston Churchill a great dislike of the manner in which Carl depicted the human race. In 1949 Marie Stopes wrote a letter to Christiansen for publication, along with her vigorously expressed intention never again to buy the newspaper 'so long as you poison it with Giles' productions'.

FAN MAIL FROM DR MARIE STOPES

Sir,

For some time past I have been increasingly disgusted, like many people, by the cartoons you publish by Giles. They degrade humanity and are very seldom funny, and their injurious effect is corrosive.

I am cancelling my order for the *Daily Express* and shall not take it again so long as you poison it with Giles' productions.

MARIE C. STOPES.
Norbury Park,
Dorking,
Surrey.

REPLY

Very well, Marie, if you're not going to take the *Express* any more because of my cartoons, I'm not going to read any more of your little books.

If Carl wasn't to be found by Christiansen and subsequent editors in the smoky, claustrophobic gloom of Poppins, he could be located, as often as not, in El Vino's, the so-called wine bar opposite the law courts which for a century or more was the daily rendezvous of senior newspapermen.

El Vino's, a forlorn place since the newspapers moved from Fleet Street, was the twentieth-century equivalent of the old coffee house, where diarists, columnists and editors – and occasionally great thinkers – gathered to gossip, with happy, alcoholic fervour, about the way of the world, the drift of mighty events and, more often than not, the peccadilloes of their colleagues. Spirits – Scotch and soda, with a little ice and very little soda, vodka and tonic with very little tonic – were always served as doubles. A single had specifically to be asked for and was sold, much to the irritation of the barman, as half a drink, the normal

'I'm not opening these damn gates every day. Tomorrow I blow the whistle.'

Daily Express, Feb. 19th, 1963

Giles just loved to complain about the railways, usually with justification. Here, he makes fun of one of the radical cost-cutting notions of the notorious Dr Beeching, the man brought in by the Government to re-shape Britain's rail network. He was also obsessed with the inconvenience of level crossings.

84

'If you've never met this Christine Keeler why the nervous rush to the phone every time it rings?'
Sunday Express, June 9th, 1963

This was the summer which was dominated, week after week, by the Profumo affair, the scandal involving John Profumo, Secretary of State for War, and temptress Christine Keeler. It slowly became clear that Miss Keeler had enjoyed numerous other secret entanglements with married gentlemen around the shires.

tariff having to be divided on the ancient till by two.

Most El Vino regulars would arrive at about one o'clock, lunchtime, and would stay until they were asked to leave, a girl with a broom sweeping up the horrible litter of fag ends, at about ten past three. Assuming that one round had been purchased every quarter of an hour, this implied that each spirit drinker had knocked back at least eight, if not nine, large tots of whisky or gin. Those who had thus consumed this impressive amount of alcohol would then go back to their newspaper offices, sit at their typewriters and proclaim to the world. Their words would appear in

'What's it worth if I let you stick on?'

Daily Express, April 4th, 1946

Horse-racing was in Giles' blood, and here is one of his early cartoons on the subject. This one refers to the Grand National and the infamous Becher's Brook.

**'Tell them to forget about the ladies at the Commonwealth Arts Festival dancing in their birthday suits—
on jumpers at once!'**

Daily Express, Sept. 14th, 1965

Here Giles' skill in animation is put to superb use.

print the following morning for the consumption of fifty million people. No one ever complained.

A similar routine would occur in the evening.

This was the old Fleet Street. Nowadays, for the record, journalists tend to work in smoke-free zones, go jogging at lunchtime and sip Perrier water as they attend their word processors. They are healthy, of course. And, old ghosts might complain, catastrophically boring.

The El Vino's of those days offered a raucous, usually articulate conviviality. The place was a gentlemen's club for heavy boozers where the few inevitable drunks were held upright by sheer force of numbers. Into all this, from time to time, stepped Carl Giles.

Mike Molloy, editor for ten years of the *Daily Mirror* and later editor-in-chief of Mirror Group Newspapers under Robert Maxwell, remembers: 'Carl used to stand surrounded by admirers, a bit pissed, legs slightly apart, jangling coins in his pocket. In some ways he was like a well-to-do farmer who had come to visit London for the day. He always enjoyed himself tremendously.'

Says Sir John Junor, august columnist and editor for thirty-two years of the *Sunday Express*: 'Eventually Carl would go back off to Ipswich leaving us all in the most terrible state.'

Swearing was forbidden in El Vino's, not that much attention was paid to the regulation. Carl recalls an incident in 1963 or thereabouts when Derek Marks was editor of the *Daily Express*. Derek was a huge man, an intimidating figure with thick glasses known as 'Jumbo' who used to sit at a circular table near the door with his equally large friend, Victor Patrick, deputy editor of the *Sunday Express*, and others who were important enough to reside at his court. One lunchtime, remembers Carl, a pest of a man kept insisting on buying the Marks gathering a round of drinks.

'He was one of those little men who insists, uninvited, on joining in. He was hanging about the conversation. It was "Derek this and Derek that".

'When it came to Derek's turn he bought the little man a large gin and tonic. He placed it on the bar by him and said: "Sir, here is your gin and tonic. I've performed my social obligations and bought you a drink. Now fuck off."'

Beyond editors, the figure who was to dominate the life and work of Carl in those times, and the life and work of everyone else who was employed on the *Express* newspapers, was that greatest of all Tory press barons, Lord Beaverbrook (1879-1964). Despite Carl's professed politics, he was in awe.

Beaverbrook – William Maxwell Aitken – a Canadian who took his title from a country stream of his North American youth, amassed a fortune in business before coming to England in 1910. He gained control of the *Daily Express* in 1916 and the *Evening Standard* in 1923. He had begun the *Sunday Express* in 1918.

There had never been newspapers in a democracy which reflected so totally and to such effect the personality of their proprietor. Not only did the journals trumpet Beaverbrook's grand imperialist views but they sparkled with his mischief and his fascination for gossip. Beaverbrook was a diminutive, 'nut-brown' little man who spoke in short, abrupt, often unintentionally comical sentences and who was famous for his notes, penned entirely as he spoke, to his staff.

Carl, as he did with everyone in power, communicated with Beaverbrook in cartoon. He sent the 'Beaver', as a birthday greeting, a humorous drawing.

Lord Beaverbrook replied, from his home, Cherkley, in Leatherhead:

May 26, 1963

My dear Giles,

I have received quite a lot of birthday cards. Some are quite beautiful. Some are not so beautiful. They are in a salver in my house here.

But I am not putting your letter in the salver. For any Giles original is much too precious to be treated in such a way. And this is a particularly excellent one.

I enjoy you in reproduction regularly. Now I have this greeting for my private pleasure and amusement. And I send you my warm thanks.

Yours sincerely...

There were other notes from Beaverbrook. But there

'It's too bad of Mr. Wilson to keep us all in this state of nervous tension about the election date.'

Sunday Express, Feb. 27th, 1966

Harold Wilson was to win the General Election at the end of March 1966 with an overall majority for Labour of 96. Election silliness hasn't changed a bit; for while the newspapers declare to their readers that the country is at fever pitch, most of the nation couldn't give a damn. Giles' Family are no different.

was none which touched Carl as deeply as that which arrived following the death of his mother.

Dear Giles,

I was very sorry indeed to hear of the death of your mother.

It is a sad loss for you. The death of parents is one of the most bitter blows in life. There is an emptiness which can never be filled. But in many happy memories there are many hours of comfort.

My warmest sympathy to you.

Yours sincerely...

Carl adored his parents. He was present when both of them died. His mother passed away quietly in an Ipswich hospital as Carl sat by her bed. Carl's father had anticipated the end and made a gift to his talented and loving young son moments before his death in an upstairs room at the family home.

Says Carl: 'He had called me upstairs and I was sitting by him. He gave me his watch. Then he just went to sleep. I was devastated. I adored him.'

Despite Lord Beaverbrook's appreciation of Carl's work, he saw little of him socially and his communications were rare. What a contrast there was in the attitude of Beaverbrook's son Max Aitken, the glamorous, much-acclaimed former Battle of Britain fighter pilot who was to take control of the Beaverbrook empire when his father died in 1964. There is one story in

Giles pictured here with his mother.

Giles' much-loved father.

'But not you, mate. Empty salmon tins and old boots are about your top score.'

Daily Express, March 29th, 1966

The World Cup, stolen from an exhibition in Westminster Hall and subsequently the subject of a ransom demand to the Football Association, was found a week later in a South London garden by a mongrel called Pickles.

'I know somewhere else where they could cut down on immigrants—this house on Sunday afternoon.'

Sunday Express, Feb. 25th, 1968

The immigration debate was raging away, not least in the Family's household.

particular which illustrates both Aitken's apparent affection for Carl and his ability to act with that kind of extravagant flamboyance which is now entirely associated with another Fleet Street age.

Aitken and Carl, tycoon's son and former Cockney scallywag, had become close socially. They shared a passionate love of sailing and an enjoyment in one another's company, though it is almost certain that

'Faster, Bert—he's gaining on you.'

Sunday Express, Dec. 19th, 1967

Giles combines his ability to depict snow scenes with his profound distaste for traffic wardens.
Most of the snow in this cartoon is simply blank paper.

Giles enjoyed a close friendship with Lord Beaverbrook's son, Max Aitken. Sir Max, who succeeded his father but declined to take his title, was as interested in having a good time as he was in newspapers. He and Giles shared a passion for yachting, as did the third figure in the picture, the then leader of the Tory Opposition, Edward Heath. The three, here seen in merry mood, were attending the 1969 Yachtsman of the Year luncheon at the Carlton Towers Hotel. Ted Heath is seen receiving this coveted honour.

Aitken, not one of the publishing world's most kindly or sensitive figures and a man, indeed, who had advocated shooting German pilots hanging from their parachutes so that they could not live to fly again, combined his affection for Carl with a powerful sense of his employee's value.

Carl, who was to own his own yachts up on the River Deben in Suffolk, occasionally crewed for Aitken down in the Solent. He would stay at the Aitken home in Cowes, a former tavern called the Prospect of Whitby, and would be invited to take part in offshore races. Carl's enjoyment of Max Aitken survived what was obviously an often unsettling and sometimes brutal experience.

'He was a brilliant sailor,' says Carl. 'But he was an absolute bastard of a skipper.' Those who have scrambled about a tilting deck underneath the thunderclapping terror of hundreds of square feet of sail to the savage curses of a tough helmsman will sympathise. The more

'*What time does the next mail train full of fivers come through?*'

Daily Express, Feb. 6th, 1969

The hilarity concerning the 1963 Great Train Robbery continued for a long time. In the most audacious crime in British history, a well–organised gang hijacked a train and escaped with mailbags of used notes worth well in excess of £2 million – today worth at least ten times as much – which were being taken away for destruction. Three years later there was an auction of Train Robbers' memorabilia.

**'They're signing a two-day truce with Grandma. They won't play any Christmas jokes on her if
she promises she won't sing.'** *Daily Express, Dec. 24th, 1968*

A Christmas truce!

fragile souls take such abuse in a deeply personal manner and worry about the humiliation for weeks afterwards.

'He was a Captain Bligh,' says Carl. 'I hated sailing with him.'

In London, enjoying the more civilised stability of dry land, Aitken and Carl would regularly lunch together at the Hyde Park Hotel, a huge establishment at the end of Piccadilly owned by the family business. One day Aitken asked Carl to go for a walk. This was much in the Beaverbrook tradition. Employees were

always being required to walk in the park with the 'old man' and Aitken took the same pleasure as his father.

'I went along,' said Carl. 'Max insisted it was good for you. So I had to. But I couldn't see much point in walking when there were better things to do.'

The two men eventually found themselves outside Jack Barclay's of Piccadilly, the celebrated automobile showroom through whose polished plate-glass window there shone in dull, tasteful splendour the bonnets and grilles of the world's most beautiful motor cars.

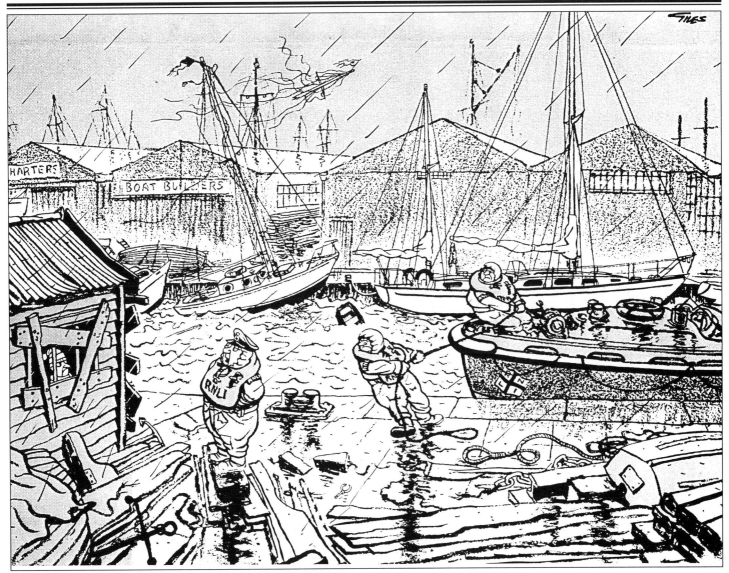

'Your wife nailing you and your boat up for Easter is hardly a case for calling out the RNLI.'

Daily Express, April 24th, 1973

Giles, who is an honorary governor of The Royal National Lifeboat Institution, has raised through his drawings millions of pounds for this fine organisation.

Each year, with a great sense of affection, he does a Christmas card for them. He looks upon lifeboatmen as the noblest of breeds.

'Come on, Sir—
admit you hate
me.'

Daily Express,
April 8th, 1971

*British Rail works
to rule. Giles uses
his talent for per-
spective to make
us feel, almost,
that the locomotive
is bursting from
the picture.*

'We went in and I left Max talking to Jack Barclay while I wandered around looking at the cars. Then Max called me over and said: "If you were to chose one for yourself, which would it be?" I pointed to a black Bentley Continental. "That would be my choice, Max," I said.

'Max then said: "Have you got a return ticket to Ipswich?" I told him I had. "Give it to me," he said. I did so. "Right," he said. "I'll keep this and you go home in that." And he pointed at the Continental. He then just walked out and was gone.

'I didn't believe it was happening.

'Then Jack Barclay said: "You're a very lucky young man. He's just bought it for you."

'Never mind what your radio said about all trains running late—mine got in bang on time an hour and a half ago.'
Daily Express, April 11th, 1972

British Rail still going slow.

'I remember arriving back in Ipswich and visiting every pub I knew. Later, as I drove slowly round one corner, two policemen actually raised their helmets as I went by.'

It was about this time in the sixties that Hugh Cudlipp attempted to lure Carl to the *Daily Mirror*. 'He showed great interest at first,' says Cudlipp. 'But, in the end, there seemed to be nothing that would persuade him to leave the *Express*.'

Max Aitken, with his sailor's nostrils, would only

'Here comes one—on your marks.'
(Department of Utter Joy. A motorist was fined £40 for turning his hose on a traffic warden)

Daily Express, March 25th, 1977

Such is Giles' dislike of traffic wardens that some might feel that counselling is the answer. In Giles' case, when *you think of it, such a course of action isn't necessary. His therapy lies in his pen.*

have had to have sniffed even the faintest pale odour of interest from the *Mirror*'s Holborn Circus headquarters at the back of Fleet Street in order to have taken some kind of swift and decisive action. But whether the gift of the Continental was in any way related to the fear of a potentially poaching rival will never be known.

While Carl's visits to Fleet Street were infrequent, and not often resulting in the present of an emperor's motor car, many of them were associated with mischief of some kind. There was one extraordinary incident, apparently entirely missing from the archives of that great newspaper parish, which involved a private film project of Carl's. The film was to be called *The Ugly Duckling* and was largely shot in and around the Giles home, Hillbrow Farm.

Carl wanted to include a sequence in London where a duck was seen walking from one side of Fleet Street, outside the *Daily Express*, under the moving traffic of Number 73 buses, taxis and so on, and out safely to the opposite pavement. Carl, anticipating a high mortality rate, had brought a number of identical ducks in cardboard boxes. Not all survived the location filming.

It is not the happiest of anecdotes and offers an uneasy association between the real Giles and those little monsters of his drawings who attach fireworks to cats. Whatever else, it serves to illustrate Carl's rather robust, farming attitude. Carl, at the time, was a pig farmer and actively participated in the various responsibilities concerning the husbandry of his 290 acres. He had, following his forebears, become a genuine East Anglian man of the land. His life in Suffolk, an astonishingly full, varied and often bizarre existence, would have been quite beyond the comprehension of the passing drunken hack in El Vino.

During the sixties, Carl, who received an OBE in 1959, found himself gradually adopted as a kind of cartooning court jester to the royal family. He amused them through cartoons and personal drawings. He would send sketches to mark various incidents and royal events and would receive delighted letters in return. The notes would begin, 'The Queen has commanded me to thank you...' and would then continue, through dictation to her private secretary, in an often informal jaunty manner in which the sovereign would join in the joke.

In the summer of 1962, Carl was invited to lunch at Buckingham Palace, though the manner in which he initially responded to this approach from Her Majesty was certainly the most outrageously rude social rebuttal that the Queen – or any monarch before her – must ever have suffered. The jester, whose ill manners were entirely unintended, was lucky not to have his ears cut off.

Prince Philip had publicly called the *Daily Express* a 'bloody awful' newspaper, in response to which Carl drew that now celebrated cartoon, showing Lord Beaverbrook being taken off to the Tower.

The insult from Prince Philip caused much amusement throughout the land and anyone who worked for and was proud of that temporarily disgraced journal was given a very hard time of it. At a Licensed Victuallers banquet at the Cavendish Hotel, Felixstowe, Carl was teased ruthlessly throughout the evening. Everybody who made a speech included references to the 'bloody awful' newspaper and those sitting adjacent to Carl would lean towards him, faces glowing with fine claret, and observe: 'We could have told Prince Philip that years ago.' Carl became less and less amused. The *Express*, after all, was his Palladium.

The following day, back home at the farm, the telephone rang and a voice announced: 'Hello, Buckingham Palace here.'

'Fuck off,' said Carl and slammed the receiver into its cradle. He had assumed, of course, that this was yet another chum calling to take him to merry task over Prince Philip. Half an hour later the telephone rang again and a nervous voice repeated: 'It's Buckingham Palace here.'

The receiver was poised to be sent crashing down as

before when something at the back of Carl's mind urged caution. 'Hello,' he said carefully. The chap on the line was, as it turned out, the Queen's man himself. He seemed very intimidated by what had occurred, remembers Carl; he had quite obviously never been thus abused in the whole of his life. 'He probably didn't know what it meant,' commented Carl.

When the Queen's equerry had established safe

'The Express is a bloody awful newspaper,' said the Duke. 'Ah, well,' said Lord B., as they trotted him off to the Tower,'at least he takes it or he wouldn't know it was a bloody awful newspaper.' Daily Express, March 22nd, 1962

Carl's drawing of his boss, Lord Beaverbrook, being led to the Tower of London caused immense amusement, both at the Daily Express *and at Buckingham Palace. Prince Philip had called the* Express *a 'bloody awful newspaper'.*

Giles poked fun at the situation, confident that he would not be sacked for cheek. Beaverbrook roared with laughter. And there was a request from the palace for the original.

WELCOME HOME

Sunday Express, May 16th, 1954

The Queen had just returned from her lengthy Commonwealth tour in 1954. The original of this cartoon was requested by Buckingham Palace.

conduct on the telephone, on this second time of calling, he explained that he merely wished respectfully to ask Carl if Her Majesty might have the original of the Beaverbrook/Tower of London cartoon to remind her of one of her husband's 'more glorious indiscretions'. Furthermore, would Mr Giles like to join the Queen, some short time in the future, for luncheon?

Carl accepted, of course. But while he was happy to establish an informal relationship with the royals through cheeky cartoonery, the idea of meeting the Queen face to face – for lunch at the palace, of all things – was utterly terrifying. 'I have never been very good in the presence of the great,' says Carl. 'I was filled with absolute dread.'

The day of the lunch arrived and Carl peered through the windscreen of the taxi as it bore him down the Mall. There, ahead, was Buckingham Palace, an edifice of unparalleled magnificence which he had sketched, often, in characteristically immaculate architectural detail, with guardsmen at their posts, corgis peeking through windows, the royal standard

'We popped our heads up to have our picture taken by Prince Philip and got two barrels off Lord Snowdon.'

Daily Express, Oct. 5th, 1961

Prince Philip asked Giles for the original of this one. The joke concerns the fact that Prince Philip had taken up photography and the celebrated Royal photographer, Lord Snowdon, had taken up shooting.

hanging lazily from its pole. It was a place you drew in cartoons and saw on postcards, not an address you arrived at for luncheon. It was certainly not a place of rendezvous which might be expected to involve a former ruffian of Chalkie's class of '28.

'I went to a side entrance and was met by this very courteous man who led me along endless corridors and showed me into this small circular anteroom overlooking the gardens at the back. There was a group of people and we were all given drinks just as if we were at home.

'Then the Queen came in with Prince Philip.'

'Ask his Royal Highness to come to my office when he's finished his solo flight.'

Daily Express, Jan. 16th, 1969

Prince Charles has the original of this one. This cartoon marks Charles' time at Trinity College, Cambridge, where the Master (in the centre) was R.A. Butler.

'Didn't you read? Princess Anne's passed her heavy goods vehicle driving test.'

Daily Express, Oct. 15th, 1974

Princess Anne has this one. Giles had long established himself as a kind of court jester to royalty.

There was always something comical about the notion of newspaper people meeting the Queen. The royal family and the fourth estate have never enjoyed anything more than an uneasy truce, even when the relationship has been at its most fleetingly encouraging. Bob Edwards, while at the *Sunday Mirror*, was among those editors summoned by the sovereign shortly after the marriage of Diana to the Prince of Wales, in order to be asked to moderate their attacks on the plainly distressed young bride.

Edwards recalls: 'As the Queen moved from one group towards another, those approached went into an unnatural, rigid pose, looking suddenly as if they could do with the attentions of an osteopath.'

Carl admits to being initially mute with terror. 'As soon as she started to talk I was put at my ease,' he says. 'She took off one shoe while she was talking – just like women do – and rubbed the other ankle with her instep.'

It is an intriguing recollection. Almost anyone who

'My advert didn't say anything about luxury. It said six-berth accommodation for the Jubilee, stone's throw from the Palace, Continental visitors welcome.'

Sunday Express, June 5th, 1977

This is another cartoon in Prince Philip's collection and refers to the Queen's Silver Jubilee in 1977.

has met the Queen in similar circumstances makes the same observation. It is almost as if the monarch uses this suburban cocktail party footwork as a carefully designed act of body language to remove fear.

'There were about half a dozen corgis running about,' says Carl, 'in a completely uncontrolled state. They were everywhere about your feet. Suddenly the Queen shouted, very loudly, "HEP". It was like a bark from a sergeant major. It made me jump. The corgis immediately stood to attention. Then filed out of the room.'

After returning home to Ipswich, Carl drew a private sketch showing the ankles of those who had attended the lunch with torn and tattered corgi-savaged trouser bottoms. He sent the drawing to the Queen.

It was the kind of mischief which only a jester might have hoped to get away with.

'Damn Joneses—he's wearing a WHITE tie!' **Daily Express, June 6th, 1977**

The country spilled out into one huge street party for most of the summer of that Jubilee year. Some went to *more extravagant lengths. Prince Philip asked for this one too.*

'HRH is in one of his doom-watch moods this morning—hear that rude little word from below when you muffed that?'

Sunday Express, Oct. 30th, 1977

The Queen has this one in her collection.

Carl received an answer from the palace in which Her Majesty expressed pleasure at the fact that 'to the best of her knowledge' Mr Giles had not lost so much as 'a shred' of his trousers. It concluded that she was 'as delighted to possess the drawing of what didn't happen at the luncheon as she is relieved that it didn't in fact happen'.

Carl's role as jester was established.

Thereafter, the royals were to receive regular cartoons – never published anywhere and all hanging on walls in private quarters – to mark various events and celebrations. On one occasion Carl sent a note to the Queen's private secretary, Martin Charteris, accompanying a drawing of members of the family, with an apology concerning the precise accuracy of the caricatures. Charteris replied on behalf of the Queen and passed on the message, placed in quotes to signify verbatim reportage, that the Queen thought them 'not half bad'.

The phrase is an amusing example of how the Queen loves to slip into what she regards as a relaxed, colloquial manner of speaking.

'The show must go on...'

Daily Express, Nov. 19th, 1970

The Queen was delighted with this cartoon and wrote to Giles to say how amused she was. The country was suffering from more industrial unrest than it had since the General Strike and even the bookies were threatening action. Here, Giles presents the imaginary outrage of horse-owners 'coming out'. Celebrated owner Lord Rosebery heads the picket line. The sovereign is sixth in line. The original hangs in the Queen's apartments.

She even from time to time and for the purpose of amusing those in her presence breaks into dreadful Cockney, an idiosyncrasy which entertains Carl, born, as he was, within the sound of Bow Bells. It is typical of her, so it is said, to emerge from a doorway at Sandringham into drizzle and proclaim in the style of Eliza Doolittle: 'Cor, it's roining – and oi 'aven't got moi brolly.'

Carl never received a formal, impersonal note in response to his drawings. The letters were always dictated personally and, as often as not, contained a 'joke'. Carl drew a private cartoon to celebrate the Queen and Prince Philip's silver wedding party at Buckingham Palace. It showed a present from Grandma of spoons stolen from British Rail. The initials BR featured prominently. Prince Charles, who had been host of the party, wrote back: '...It was a great problem explaining the significance of "B.R." to members of the Foreign Royal Families who have not had the good fortune to travel by that exquisite mode of travel...' Railway trains, it is well known, are regarded by royals as the most unspeakably undignified way to be conveyed about the kingdom.

It is not just Carl's private sketches that hang about the royal residences. The royals have thirty-six of his originals, all requested.

The Queen has three, the best of which shows the royal barge approaching the jetty of some tropical isle from the distantly anchored royal yacht *Britannia*. It is manned by snappily saluting sailors. An able seaman has just thrown the bowline towards the jetty and missed. One tar is seen remarking out of the corner of his mouth: 'HRH is in one of his doom-watch moods this morning – hear that rude little word from below when you muffed that?'

For some years Carl was taken to royal audience, from a field behind his Suffolk farm, by helicopter. The pilot was Tommy Sopwith, a friend of Princess Alexandra. She is another enthusiastic fan and whenever she was guest for luncheon at the Hertfordshire mansion home of Dick Wilkins, the late,

colourful City stockjobber and particularly close friend of the Queen Mother, Carl would be invited to join the party. Sopwith, whose father was one of the country's greatest aviation pioneers, would clatter his machine down in Carl's meadow, chickens flying for their lives, sometimes with Prince Charles in one of the passenger seats, and run over to the house to collect Carl.

On one occasion Carl, who was fascinated by anything mechanical, became so intrigued by the controls that he discreetly and completely recklessly twisted an irresistible handle down by his seat in the co-pilot's position, which bore, in red letters, the words 'Increase' and 'Decrease'.

The knob, vital to the mysterious aerodynamic performance of helicopters, controlled climb and descent. The helicopter, only just above the fields, had still not cleared the pylons and high-tension cables which straddled Carl's estate. As Carl twitched the control, the nose of the machine dipped and the helicopter dropped with potentially catastrophic determination towards the ground.

Sopwith only just managed to retrieve the situation, the rotor blades sending a swirl of down draught over the grass as it levelled out, and was forced to fly *under* the wires. As they regained height, Sopwith raised an admonishing index finger to shoulder height and said with trembling solemnity: 'Carl, you must never do that again.'

Carl was frequently flown off to royal country lunches by Sopwith. Joan, who did not attend, would watch her husband from the kitchen window whirring away over the treetops and would quietly reflect on how things had changed from the days in Great Percy Street.

Joan has always been determined to stay in the background and has been successful in doing so. She won't even have her photograph taken with Carl if she feels there is any question of its appearing, sooner or later, in a publication. Not that Carl is ever keen on the notion himself.

'Diana—where did you put William's old pram?' Daily Express, Feb. 14th, 1984

It is announced that the Princess of Wales is pregnant with Harry. Giles uses the excuse to suggest that Charles' outhouses are just as full of junk as anyone else's. Rather curiously, Princess Michael of Kent asked for this one.

Princess Margaret, the most gregarious of the royals and a lover of parties, was particularly fond of Carl. She collected artistic people about her, but Carl was never a member of her personal court.

He was not a dancer, nor an actor, he didn't stand on his head or set the table on a roar, he was simply the chap who drew cartoons to the enduring amusement of the nation and to the especial pleasure of the royal family.

Most of Carl's work involved the ordinary people of the country. It was almost as if, when he featured the royals in his pictures, they actually felt privileged to be included.

They were certainly shameless in asking for originals of cartoons, although Carl was always happy to release them. It soon became evident, following the rapid public acclamation after he joined the *Daily Express*, that the drawings were one day going to enjoy a considerable value.

In November 1970, there was a threatened strike of

racehorse owners. Carl drew a cartoon, carried by the *Express*, showing a line-up of militant-looking racehorse owners which included a grim-faced Lord Rosebery and a truculent monarch.

Wrote the Queen's press secretary, Bill Heseltine, in November 1970: 'I am writing on behalf of the subject (only subject is, on reflection, *not* the right word) of your cartoon depicting the strike of racehorse owners... If you have not promised it elsewhere, The Queen would very much like to have it.'

It is difficult to imagine that Carl, or anyone else, would have written back saying: 'Sorry, Ma'am, but I'm saving it for a bloke at the Fountain.'

The most enthusiastic collector of Giles originals was Prince Philip. He has fifteen.

One of his favourites is the drawing of 5 October 1961, which features three young grouse, feathers blasted from their bodies and staggering about in a clearing in the heather. One of them is scratching its head and addressing the scowling parent birds. The joke concerned the rather surprising news stories of the time that photographer Lord Snowdon, then married to Princess Margaret, had taken to joining shooting parties and that Prince Philip had taken up photography. The caption read: 'We popped our heads up to have our picture taken by Prince Philip and got two barrels off Lord Snowdon.'

Prince Philip immediately contacted Carl and declared: 'Just for that you can give me the original.'

The Duke amused Carl. He seemed to indulge in a furtive anarchy, a kind of fantasy rebellion against the often absurd position he held as consort. During his meetings with Carl he would give the impression that he saw the situation about him just as Carl might see it in a cartoon.

During one garden party he nodded towards the slow-shuffling, polite though eager multitude of councillors, lollipop ladies, school matrons, church women, local newspaper editors, blimps, engine drivers and rural grandees, lady charity officials and elderly actresses. The scene bobbed, swayed and undulated with several acres of pink hats. Said Prince Philip, glancing up behind the palace roof at an angry June thunderhead: 'Wouldn't it be marvellous if it just chucked it down right now.' Carl also talks with admiration of the time that Prince Philip squirted the press with a garden hose at the Chelsea Flower Show. Kindred spirits, in a manner of speaking.

The relationship between Prince Philip and the *Express* was always strained, though no one was ever quite sure why. Prince Philip hated all of the tabloids. He did attempt to establish a truce in the earlier days by asking Lord Beaverbrook to the palace for lunch. The Beaver never went. Bob Edwards, Beaverbrook's editor of the time, recalls how he was enduring one of his many walks in St James's Park with his proprietor when Prince Philip's helicopter rose out of the walled back garden of the palace like a crimson iron grasshopper, throbbing and clattering overhead.

'Bow down, Bob,' cried the little Beaverbrook. 'Bow down before your lord and master.' The order was heavy with ill-natured irony.

The *Express*, essentially a royalist paper, was always poking spiky fun at Prince Philip and it may well be that he was aware of more than a token lack of respect. But the Duke was a good target. Sir Osbert Lancaster, the greatest pocket cartoonist of the age, had two of his upper-class, Mayfair ladies discussing Philip's crude, much-publicised demand of the time that the nation should 'pull its finger out'. Asked Sir Osbert's Maudie Littlehampton of her chum: 'Out of what is it, exactly, that Prince Philip wishes us to pull our finger?'

Still, Carl was a fan, though his favourite description of the Duke might not have been the best illustration of his often declared high esteem.

'He always looks like the man,' says Carl, 'who has called to see about the smell on the landing.'

Carl's fascination with cartoons began when he was little more than four. His father used to bring back

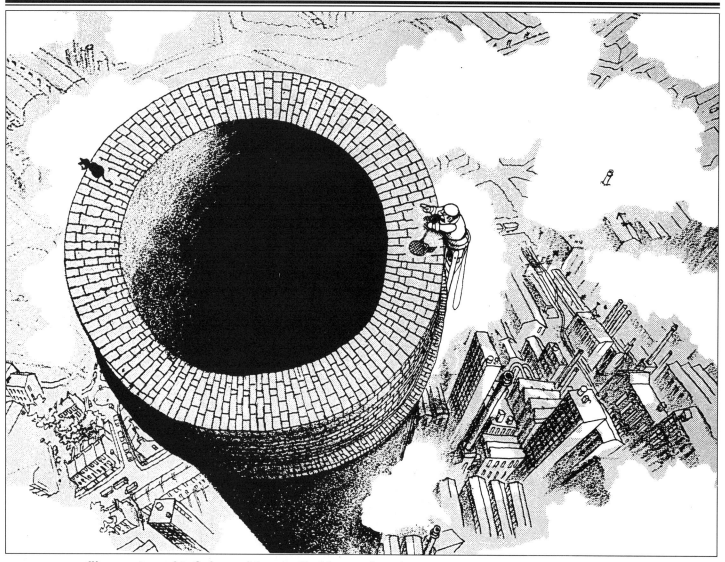

'I'm getting a bit fed up with you climbing up here just to get your picture in the papers.'

Sunday Express, Dec. 11th, 1983

Giles suspends the reader twenty feet above the dark mouth of a factory chimney. While his joke about a cat which got itself into the newspapers for its climbing activities is mildly funny, the humour is eclipsed by the feeling of terror which the picture evokes. It is an amazing drawing and should certainly be kept well away from anyone who suffers from even the mildest form of vertigo.

copies of *Tatler*, the society magazine which contained the work of Captain Bruce Bairnsfather, a serving officer who sent home from France boldly drawn sketches of life in the trenches. The young Carl used to wait with great excitement for the arrival, on a Thursday evening, of the magazine. He would sit beside the coal fire in the cosy Giles sitting room and study with great care every detail of Captain Bairnsfather's work. The sketches, wonderfully funny, would show the kind of figure who was to become such a feature of Carl's work in the Second World War, that British foot soldier as the tommy who was able, with merry and cocky good humour, to prevail in the most unthinkable circumstances. Bairnsfather was born in 1888 and died in 1959.

Later, while on *Reynolds News*, Carl's hero was Pont – Graham Laidler – who drew those typical fine-line cartoons of aristocratic and middle-class life for which the magazine was famous. The detail, remembers Carl, was exquisite and the backgrounds always full of humorous points.

Pont, who suffered from permanent ill health, died in 1940 at the age of thirty-two.

Says Carl, who admits to few other gods in his trade: 'When he went I felt I had lost a dear friend.'

Artistic inspiration and subsequent historic achievement apart, Carl Giles' life has been unashamedly devoted to pleasure. It has been a gloriously successful hedonistic odyssey, a joyful journey occasionally interrupted on the way by kitchen appliance salesmen, newspaper production executives, police patrolmen, lollipop ladies, Chalkie-faced traffic wardens and tax inspectors. Visiting Fleet Street was merely a small

diversionary part of a hectic schedule which involved motoring, yachting, DIYing, amateur film-making and, on a daily basis, merrily pubbing between the backstreet bars, country lane alehouses and waterside taverns of Suffolk, all the way from Ipswich to Felixstowe and back, and there and back again. His final foray of the day would usually start about midnight and he would seldom be home before 2.30am, often with a jolly group of companions serenading the moon and progressing unsteadily in its silvery light towards the Giles front door. Joan would usually be up in her dressing gown at the sound of their approach to place sausages under the grill.

It was in Ipswich, too, that Carl had his meticulously planned and pleasantly well-appointed private studio.

From here he produced, for half a century, three cartoons a week for his newspapers, the *Daily* and *Sunday Express*, painted his colourful yearly Christmas cards for his beloved Royal National Lifeboat Institution – of which he is life President – drew amusing menus for that charitable luncheon and dinner club, the Saints and Sinners, and created endless personal cartoons which were dispatched to chums, editors, police inspectors, bosses and to the sovereign herself.

It was in this studio that Carl's relentless pursuit of off-duty fun was regularly interrupted by six- to ten-hour periods of intense, disciplined, creative concentration. Carl would live his drawings, he would enter them. He could see round each corner, through each betting shop window. A whole life, out of sight, bustled beyond the immediate frame of his cartoon.

From this brightly lit Ipswich room above a busy high street there were dispatched over a period of fifty years, usually late and, in Carl's perfectionist view, incomplete and unsatisfactory, some 7,500 cartoons. They were, even in the first twelve months, to establish Giles as the twentieth century's most celebrated artist of the people. He has been described as a benign Hogarth.

His characters have become permanent, universally valued institutions. The most loved of his creations form the Family, and the two most enduring senior individual characters of the Giles cast are, without doubt, Chalkie and Grandma; he the skeletal schoolmaster tyrant who ruled generations of children through cane and sarcasm, she the very Empress of

'Here it comes again—they didn't call off racing just for a bit of frost when she was a girl.'

Daily Express, Feb. 20th, 1978

Grandma sturdily makes her way through the Giles snow to do battle with the racing staff over cancellation of the

day's sport. The racing types look suitably disagreeable, so the confrontation is likely to be lively.

116

battle-axe matriarchs.

There is a significant difference between the two. Chalkie is real, drawn in every single, sharply remembered respect from the Mr Chalk who terrorised Carl's schooldays; Grandma is a figure who has evolved and is not, Carl assures us, particularly based on any relative of his acquaintance.

The real Giles grandmothers were dignified late-Victorian figures who would have been horrified to have found themselves directly compared to the fierce, black-garbed ancient of their grandson's imagination. But Grandma is, insists her creator, a very much warmer, more compassionate figure than might be assumed, borrowing a few finer traits, as it were, from the real thing.

Grandma Giles – the actual Grandma Giles – was a magnificent Victorian figure, a handsome woman in black, with a bustle at her posterior and white lace about her wrists. She was a lady, so typical of that time, with poise and elegance and strength of character and with the mix of authority and kindness that command respect and discipline and, occasionally, fear. It is a long-extinct breed, surely. Today, grannies wear jeans and tight sweaters and smooch at the back of the cinema.

Says Carl: 'Grandma Giles was a church-going lady and didn't drink, although she would have the odd brandy and Guinness for medicinal purposes. She was very strict but compassionate. She had a lovely, gentle, slight smile. And she was always Grandma Giles. You would never, never call her Granny. You respected her and you certainly never took a chance with her.'

Carl, as might be expected, did eventually take a chance with her, but only when she was ultimately confined, with rheumatoid arthritis, to that safest of restrictive perches for stern grandmothers, the wheelchair. Grandma Giles,

The real thing! This is the genuine Grandma Giles whose husband, a jockey, had ridden for Edward VII. She was a fine woman, stern on occasions, but kind. She expected good behaviour and got it. However, when she was confined to a wheelchair and needed propulsion down the street she usually regretted asking grandson Giles to do the honour. He and a chum used to reach speeds for which the conveyance was not designed nor its passenger prepared.

whose husband, Alfred, the former jockey to Edward VII, had died at the age of fifty-three, lived in Myddelton Square where she was cared for by two spinster daughters. Her home was round the corner from Joan's house in Great Percy Street – Grandma Giles was, of course, also Joan's grandmother – and for a time it was the duty of Carl and his young friend Terry, Joan's brother, to push their shared matriarch from one family address to the other. This, on occasions, was done with unseemly speed, the two lads joining forces to propel the chair round Myddelton Square at least once more than was strictly necessary, at the pace of a briskly trotting horse. Grandma, as brave as they come, was plainly terrified but bore the ordeal, by all accounts, with the fortitude of her breed.

Grandma Giles was the paternal grandmother. Her counterpart, whom she never met, was Nanny Clarke, as she was known in the family – Carl's mother's mother.

A cosier, softer and jollier woman, she was altogether very different and Carl admits to having a very special affection for her, finding her company a great deal easier than that of Grandma Giles. Nanny Clarke, whose husband was a quietly spoken, peace-loving and gentlemanly insurance salesman, such as existed in those days, lived in a house in Norwich which always bustled with aunts and uncles, cousins, nephews and nieces. Carl would travel up from the Angel to visit for holidays and enjoyed it so much that he would stay on, finally attending a local school.

'Nanny Clarke,' he recalls, 'was a really colourful woman. And she liked a drink. She wasn't a drinker, in that sense, but she loved to have a glass with people. She liked the

Grandmother Clarke – known in the family as Nanny Clarke – was altogether less formal and a much jollier woman. Nanny Clarke, who was Giles' maternal grandmother, lived in Norfolk and her home was frequently visited by young Giles. There is not much about Nanny Clarke which could easily be spotted in the cartoon Grandma. Still, Giles insists that Grandma has ingredients from both of these fine ladies.

'I'm trying to work out her arithmetic—she buys a half dozen British Gas shares then leaves her gas fire on all day so they make a profit.'

Daily Express, Nov. 25th, 1986

Grandma's mathematics rightly puzzle Ernie who is tackling the problem with the help of an abacus. Here, Grandma differs from the more traditional matriarch who tends, rather, to switch things off in order to save the pennies.

feeling that an occasion was being enjoyed.

'She was far more extrovert than Grandma Giles and she had such a happy little house.'

Carl uses the word 'little' as a term of endearment. There is no other word that Carl uses so frequently to describe something or someone for whom he has deep affection.

He continued: 'But Nanny Clarke could be strict, too. Everything had to be done correctly and everyone had to have good manners and always go out properly dressed.

'And she was a courageous woman. After Grandpa Clarke died, in the twenties, there was a great economic crisis in Norfolk which followed the collapse of the shoe industry. She went out from door to door, taking up Grandpa's insurance round. And she opened up the front room of the house to sell things like dolls and dresses. She made it into a little shop.

'Whatever money she made she would spend on us all. We would get toys and she would always make sure there was a bottle of whisky in the house.'

How different these grandmothers sound from the Grandma of Carl's cartoon Family. However, he insists that some of the ingredients are there. We only have to look.

On the face of it, it is difficult to believe that any grandma could exist who is quite as formidable as the creature who developed, with whatever inspiration, from Carl's imaginings, though what she plainly represents among that particular breed is the old girl who, in dotage, determines not to go under, not to 'go gently

into that good night', but to fight to the end a fierce battle against everyone from town hall bureaucrats and dodgy bookmakers to publicans who fiddle the pint of Guinness. Perhaps, unconsciously, Carl based Grandma on himself.

It is a notion which is shared by Johnny Speight. He says: 'I have known Carl for a long time now and I have a strong suspicion he is Grandma.'

If Carl had been an old granny he would undoubtedly have been very like her. At his grumpiest and most difficult he is certainly closer to her than he is to any of his other characters. Certainly, when his mouth takes a down-turn and his glasses angrily reflect the light and his short white hair appears to bristle with irritation, all you would need to add would be a black, neck-high frock, a handbag and an umbrella and you would have Grandma.

'Grandma,' points out Carl, 'has even been known to ride a motor bike. She is aggressive – violence, perhaps, is her keynote.'

Violence, it should be said, is not a characteristic one would associate with Carl, though it may be, as in many such creative souls, that there lurks an axeman. Grandma, in that case, has been a useful agent.

So where did Grandma start, where did she come from, what was the spark to her evolution? She certainly didn't appear overnight. It was way back in the early war days while Carl was at *Reynolds News* that he reckons Grandma may have enjoyed her first appearance.

'Butch has slipped his lead and gone off to Paris for lunch.'   *Sunday Express, Nov. 4th, 1990*

Grandma and the Family quite naturally had to become involved on the day that the workmen broke through in the Channel Tunnel in 1990.

'If Grandma's bought a short dress I'm going to leave home.'

Daily Express, Jan. 31st, 1958

Here is Grandma all the way back in 1958. She's not changed much. Nor has she grown older. But neither has any other member of the Family. They are caught either in dotage or in extreme youth in a timeless world.

'Mum! Grandma's gone down behind the piano.'   *Daily Express, Dec. 28th 1974*

Grandma is game for simply anything.

Here she is, traced back to an old scrapbook, standing between a couple of tommies. She is a mischievously smiling, moon-faced little figure with just an early hint of trouble in the threatening angle of the handbag, though the suggestion of defiance is undoubtedly there in the caption. 'We say to her: "Friend or Foe?" and all she keeps saying is: "Foe!"' There is little else to link her to the later Grandma other than the flowers on the hat, flowers that were joined at some stage by a small cloth bird.

Bit by bit the face was to collapse until all that was visible under the hat's brim and over the white fur

'Her horse fell at the first fence, our cricketers are a pain in her neck, so she's off to pastures new.'

Sunday Express, April 6th, 1986

She'll be back!

round the collar of the ankle-length coat – once fox, but no longer – was a pair of National Health specs on a button nose and a large straight mouth, like a long thin slit in a black letter box. Sometimes, on occasions of great anger, it would become serrated. Sometimes, quite startlingly, it would open and develop into a huge smile. The handbag, now, has a heavy padlock and, within, a chain for attaching to the chair in the pub. The brolly with the ivory parrot's head is not really a defence against the weather. It is a rioter's weapon.

'Perhaps we all knew a grandma like that a long time ago,' says Eric Sykes. 'Or perhaps we thought we did. But nowadays grannies all look like Michelle Pfeiffer.'

This little lady, according to Giles, is his prototype Grandma. The flowers are stacked up on her head and she looks altogether jollier. This cartoon was drawn for Reynolds News *in the early part of the war.*

'If I were you, Vera, I'd get Mr. Bush and Saddam Hussein to split the bill.'

Grandma, smiling broadly, pokes fun at the pathetic Vera for becoming so overwhelmed by the stresses of the Gulf War. In the background a sinister figure is inspecting the price tag on a cane. It is Chalkie.

'Threatening football referees is one thing—slapping Flower Show judges because you didn't get a Highly Commended is another!'

Here is the handbag in action. Note Grandma's derisory entry to the Chelsea Flower Show.

EPSOM

The bookie characters are so right in this cartoon, though it is doubtful that punters would be permitted to keep them attached to the end of a heavy length of chain.

Grandma's use of extreme measures to protect her investments at race meetings seldom seem to draw much attention from the crowds.

The fun of the Giles annuals covers is that the joke is shared by front and back. A story is told. The two pictures here are a good example of Giles' intricate brick and stone work. (1970)

Those who have studied Giles closely will almost certainly be able to anticipate from the front cover what will be happening on the back. Note that amid all the frantic noise and terror George the bookworm is still deep in his volume of Proust or whatever. (1968)

This tells a jolly little story. The sequence has a touch of the animator's art. Here once again we observe Giles' keen awareness of social divisions in the Army; the privates on the bench are delighted to see the sergeant major getting his comeuppance from a superior officer.

Grandma in rare defeat. Note the ever-present Stinker with his camera. Stinker is otherwise known as Larry and is the friend of the younger members of the family. (1985)

Giles has achieved an extraordinarily realistic lighting effect here. And note the detail of the equipment; home movie-making is another of Giles' hobbies. (1972)

Giles in splendidly anarchic mood. The spikey-haired ruffian, Stinker, abandons his camera in favour of mines. (1965)

Here Giles links up with Lewis Carroll. Note the timid Vera's terror. (1973)

Every leaf has been drawn here. (1979)

For a movie effect it is worth focusing on Ernie (holding the rope at the corner of the blanket in the right-hand picture) and then looking very quickly at Ernie in the second drawing. Whoosh, the blanket's gone and Ernie has taken up that wonderful circus performer's pose. (1975)

Grandma, in earmuffs, appears to have masterminded this disaster. Note the money changing hands at the bottom right-hand corner of the cartoon. (1978)

Still, it matters little if Grandma is a period figure; she has proved, literally, to be indestructible and indispensable. On a number of occasions Carl has threatened to kill her off but has had his hand stayed by a roar of national protest, particularly from the young. Grandma, of course, like the children in Giles cartoons, represents the force of anarchy. No wonder she's loved by youth. Whatever else, Grandma is the true mega-star of the Giles Palladium show. And she's there for ever. She is, after all, Britannia.

Immortality, too, is the fate of that schoolmaster of everyone's nightmares, Chalkie, though he and Grandma seem seldom to meet. It is as if each has a healthy respect for the other and keeps a distance. However, the skull-headed Mr Chalk has made a brief appearance from time to time in the vicinity of the old girl.

One rather chilling cartoon shows Grandma and the snivelling family member, Vera, in a chemist's shop, the latter buying pills to cope with the migraines, backaches, sore throats and tensions brought about by the stress of the Gulf War.

Spookily, and inexplicably, we see the unmistakable figure of Chalkie in the background. He is closely examining canes.

Grandma is a familiar figure to the citizens who pass through that bustling corner of London, the Angel, Islington. There is a pub there, close to where her creator was born, called The Giles. Grandma magnificently adorns its sign.

And then there is the Family. Plain Vera, with the constant cold, nose dripping and the never ceasing supply of tablets, is married to George the bookworm, a pipe-smoking, tranquil figure, familiar to most families, who simply never notices the noise and chaos which permanently disrupt the domestic world about him. Vera and George have the baby, George Junior, who occasionally writes illiterate notes covered with ink blots.

There are Father and Mother, of course, and they have the three girls, grown-up Ann and Carol and youngest daughter Bridget with the pigtails and gymslip. The young son is Ernie, who is a miniature version of his father and who is usually equipped with an unpleasant weapon of some kind. Finally, there are the twins, Laurence and Ralph – named after actors Sir Laurence Olivier and Sir Ralph Richardson – an identical pair of mites who constantly strain at the double leash held by their mother, Ann – the father is unknown – and who, like so many Giles characters, appear in forward motion always to be two or three inches above the ground.

Carl was once prevailed upon to draw the family tree; it includes Randy the goldfish, Rush the dopey, confused dog, and Natalie the cat.

George Junior

Vera

George

Mother

Father

Bridget

Ernie

Carol

Ann

The twins, Laurence and Ralph

130

THE GILES FAMILY TREE

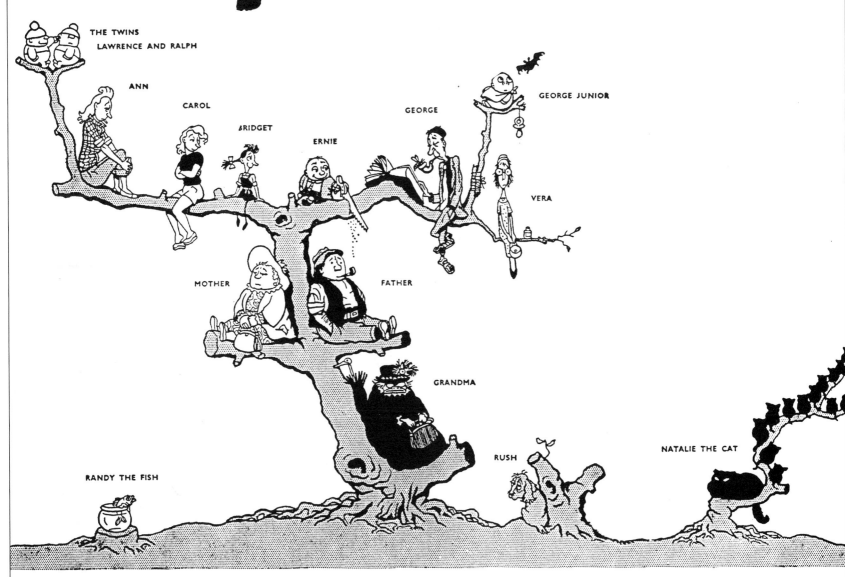

'You've bought Grandma a WHAT for Christmas?'

Sunday Express, Dec. 21st, 1980

There is much enjoyable detail in this cartoon but it is the expression on Mum's face and the rest of the body language, including the toes of her Wellington boots slightly turned in, which brings the moment so marvellously to life. Both the twins, it will be noticed, have already been bitten quite severely. Butch, the dog, is utterly disconsolate.

'There you are! You didn't think we would let you spend Father's Day on your own.'

Sunday Express, June 16th, 1985

Poor Father. He has spent many weeks looking forward to his first day's coarse fishing. Approaching him across the field is what can only be described as a fisherman's most fearful nightmare. Ernie is actually blowing a trumpet while the twins are crashing cymbals. Grandma is driving a C5, that dotty invention of Sir Clive Sinclair.

'How come a Great Dane bit a Crown Court Judge and got off with a pat on the head, yet Butch gets porridge for eating a couple of Grandma's Christmas cards?'

Sunday Express, Dec. 21st, 1975

Many of Giles' activities occur in the suburban back garden. It is a world of old bicycle wheels, long abandoned toys, unmown grass, shed, dog-house and dustbins. Porridge, in this case, means prison, of course.

'Mum, you know the new extension Dad's building himself to save massive builder's bills?'

Sunday Express, March 2nd, 1975

The detail in this cartoon makes it quite clear that the artist is himself a DIY expert. Giles, in his own well-equipped workshop in Suffolk, has proved himself to be more professional than amateur. He would certainly have the knowledge to avert such an appalling catastrophe as has occurred here.

Writer and art critic William Feaver studied the thirty-ninth *Giles Annual* over Christmas 1985 and wrote the following appraisal: 'The highlights of the Giles year are unchanging. Christmas is the season of excessive paper chains. The *Daily Express* Boat Show follows (joke about Dad as seafaring type buying a festive mop for the wife), then Mother's Day – Dad trips over cat, sends surprise breakfast-in-bed flying – then the Derby (Grandma again blowing her pension on Lester Piggott). The summer hols are spent in hut 14,002 on a windy coast. The perennially pre-teen, ex-St Trinian's Bridget is distressed at Boy George's reported change in hairstyle. A gull settles in Grandma's hat.

'1985 began, naturally, with aunts and parents sleeping off the old year in front of the telly; all but Vera's lugubrious husband, George, still deep in his Orwell. George, who usually affects a beret, is lost without a book, preferably something by Sartre.'

The Giles Family, in prototype form, first appeared on 5 August 1945, in a *Sunday Express* cartoon captioned 'It's quicker by rail.'

For the next two years the Family developed and extended.

Wrote Feaver: 'Like the Archers, the Huggetts, the Dixons, the Glums, the Garnetts and the Ogdens – who all owe something to them – the Gileses are not so much your typical English family as a family around whom everything revolves. They are provincial but come up to town quite a bit – the Boat Show and so on – and travel a good deal. Their credibility depends largely on the accuracy of the settings.'

Feaver, from his brief study of a year in the life of the Family, describes an event on a sunny day in June. It captures splendidly the very nature of the Giles Family, the inseparable mix of domestic affection and horror.

'Sunday June 16 and Dad slips away on his own for a bit of coarse fishing. Hardly has he settled down with thermos and sandwiches in the shade of a burly Giles willow when across the meadow come Mum and Bridget, Ernie sounding his trumpet, the twins with their cymbals, George with baskets, Vera with her hanky and Grandma, ahead of the field in her Sinclair C5. He should have known: it's Father's Day.'

But it is not simply the central joke or even the many little subplots which we remember; it is more often, as in great art, the mood and the weather and the detail, the grassy bank of the river under the willow touched with splashes of bright summer sunshine through which birds flit.

Somehow you know that it is mid-afternoon and it's hot and it's still and a dog can be heard barking a mile away. You hear the river chuckling and gurgling and hear the cuckoo and the woodwind fluting of the pigeons.

Says Feaver: 'The excuse for the joke is often less effective than the placing: dour wintry sky over the station approach; mud at low tide; juggernauts churning the slush; double yellow lines leading from traffic warden to traffic warden. No one is more used to conveying in tone and scribble the precise textures of pebbledash and privet.'

And in Giles' winter pictures, what other artist could create so simply and without apparent effort those astonishing snow scenes, the churchyard with monstrous choirboys hiding behind a gravestone, an ammunition pyramid of hard snowballs in readiness, awaiting the hurrying distant figure of the unsuspecting parson in his surplice.

It is a late December afternoon and light shafts out through stained-glass windows of the church. It is bitter. It is grey and gloomy and very, very cold; there is a soft quietness, and everything in sight is covered with three inches of freshly fallen snow.

Says Mike Molloy, an artist before he rose through the editorial ranks of the Mirror Group: 'He was able to create a snow scene simply by leaving areas and patches of his picture blank on a rough textured board and adding the simplest stroke with a wax pencil.'

'We've been tobogganing—Dad's in Ward 10 but the sledge is all right.'

Sunday Express, Dec. 3rd, 1978

The snow has fallen on suburbia and Mother collects the coal. One of the effects of Giles' frequent snow scenes is that, such is their realism, you feel that someone has suddenly opened a window before you on a bleak winter's day. The picture actually seems to cause a drop in the temperature.

'Nothing's going to stop him giving the lawn its Easter haircut with his new mower.'

Sunday Express, March 30th, 1975

Snow. And Grandma helps out. It is the blizzard effect in the corners of the windows and on the ledges which help to give the drawings a startlingly life-like effect.

Here is a picture of Giles, taken in January 1987, standing in real snow. In the background a helicopter has arrived to collect the following Sunday's cartoon from the weather-bound artist.

'A few burst pipes and a power cut pack 'em in better'n all the sermons, eh, Vicar?'

Sunday Express, Feb. 5th, 1956

The curious thing about Giles' winter scenes is that the snow always appears only just to have stopped. It still clings to the trees and lies virgin on the ground.

'Dad—he's pinching our coal.'

Sunday Express, Dec. 24th, 1950

And Christmases, of course, are always white.

'Oh dear, now we really are on the brink of World War 3—he's out first ball of the season.'

Sunday Express, April 27th, 1980

When it's not snowing in Giles' England it tends to be pouring with rain. He manages the effect of wetness with the same skill that he creates a landscape of freshly fallen snow. Here is all the misery of cricket in the rain.

Jak, the acclaimed cartoonist of the *Evening Standard*, who admits to being a disciple of Giles, agrees. 'Carl had this flair for leaving things out. With bricks, for example, he would leave most of them out where I would have put every one of them in. I would draw a Norman arch and he would draw the effect of a Norman arch and his would be better, his would look more effective.'

Jak was an admirer of Giles, an artist who was much influenced by him, but he also wanted his job. In later years he would say to Jocelyn Stevens, the managing director of Beaverbrook Newspapers, the group which then incorporated the *Evening Standard:* 'Come on, Jocelyn, when are you going to get rid of Giles and let me take over?'

Stevens admonished him. He replied: 'How would you feel if one day someone were to ease you out?'

Recalls Jak: 'He was quite right. Anyway, I never did take over. And I will always have a tremendous admiration for Carl's work, although I felt he coasted a bit in later years.

'He used to treat me with great caution. I once said to him – joking – that whenever I was short of an idea I would get down an old *Giles Annual*.

'I learned a few days later that he had complained about me. He had registered a strong objection to me nicking his ideas. He could be very difficult, you know. He was always "resigning".

'Still, he was a bloody genius. I think they should have given him a knighthood. The royal family thought he was marvellous, didn't they? I wonder why he never got one.'

One newspaper knight who was a particular fan of Giles and who would no doubt agree with Jak was television's most distinguished former newsreader and ex-editor of the *Daily Express*, Sir Alastair Burnet. He observed amusingly: 'Gilesland is, as everyone knows, a country wholly surrounded by choppy seas and duffers in boats.

'Its pastures are peopled by idle cattle, idle farm hands and even idler earls. No snow falls there that does not end up impacting on the necks of vicars and postmen. No rain falls that does not raise the grass for the lawnmower industry.

'It is not a democracy, but an anarchy, the urban guerrillas led by a gerontic Passionara in black. Its pubs never close, its butlers never falter. Its men are pitiable but persevering, its women patient in their superiority, its children numerous. It is full of mischief. We have to shout on *News At Ten* to make ourselves heard above the Gilesland hubbub.'

It is a glorious and unquestionably accurate notion.

Most appreciations of Carl's art concern his work for the *Daily Express*. Sadly, some of his earlier material seems to have disappeared for ever. But he offers one example of a pre-war *Reynolds* cartoon which he says illustrates a period when he was still 'searching for a style'. He was scarcely twenty at the time.

The drawing shows a tramcar which has been stopped, as it evidently has been before, by a lady's washing on the overhead electric cable. There are a few Giles clues, but not many. Note the expression of amused resignation on the face of the tram driver. See the upturned feet on one pair of longjohns and the patch in the bottom of the other. There is the Giles signature but even that has yet to acquire its characteristic slope.

What is pure early Giles is the subject matter. Trams. He loved drawing them. He adored them and they appeared, while they still clattered and squeaked along our city streets and, in particular, around the eight-line junction outside his home at the Angel, in many of his cartoons. He has said: 'Oh, and the smell, when you got a shower of rain on the dusty streets and the smells came up like an orchestra, the trams and the oil on the rails and the electricity transformers. Lovely, lovely!'

It was soon after those days of half a century ago that John Gordon, the editor of the *Sunday Express*, spotted Carl's work in *Reynolds* and, after some persuading, lured him to Beaverbrook Newspapers.

'Heaven knows our game could do with a streaker, but I'm not sure Vicar's good lady wife is quite streaker material.'

Sunday Express, June 8th, 1986

The streaking vicar's wife causes mayhem on the pitch. Note what has happened to the wicketkeeper.

Gordon wrote in the first ever annual of Giles' work: 'I think that in his own particular line of cartoon Giles is without an equal in Britain today. Indeed, I know no better in all of the world.

'He has that greatest of all gifts of genius, the common touch. He knows the common people, their troubles, their foibles, their joys, their aspirations. He is, in fact, the common man.

'But he is something more than the great cartoonist. Study his work closely and you will find that he is a great artist as well. His backgrounds are perfect in structure, in detail and in balance.

'And finally, the people in his cartoons, those odd children and those even odder grown-ups. When I looked at them first I laughed at them, but was inclined to say: "They are amusing but they are certainly not people." But I was wrong. I know it now. For whenever I pass along the street I look at the people and say: "After all Giles is right. Every face is a Giles face." Try it for yourself.'

There have been many tributes to Giles' work over the years but there would seem to have been none which was as perceptive as that of the late prima

'Your turn today Reginald—I told her about it yesterday.'

This strange little cartoon appeared in Giles' early Reynolds News *days. Giles admits that at this point he was still searching for a style. He had always loved trams but there are one or two other clues. See the expression on the tram driver's face, the upturned leggings on the clothes line and the solitary sock. Interestingly, the Giles signature has not even started to develop a flourish.*

ballerina, Dame Margot Fonteyn.

She said: 'Very few men can see clearly all the imperfections of face and form in the world around yet still retain an indulgent affection for humanity.

'Such a person is Carl Giles. He must be a very compassionate man.

'Anyone else with his needle-sharp eyes would find it hard not to be biting in the humour, but he mocks us only very gently. Even his most horrible characters are to some extent endearing.

'We laugh at them but also more often *with* them and sympathise with their plight. We can feel for all of them even when they are absolutely humourless and stupid.

'It always seems to me that my favourites are his children – those little no-necked monsters that reveal all the characteristics of the adults they will become, although it is noticeable that their faces are never completely stupid.

'They always show a natural intuition and vitality and there seems to be much more going on inside their busy little heads than in some of the self-satisfied grown-ups, spoiled perhaps by the influences of civilisation.

'Which is the one you say is a grossly overpaid old crow?'

Sunday Express, May 19th, 1974

Giles loved drawing nurses and was constantly amused by scenes in hospital. However, while he supported their cause for better pay he could, on occasions, be a little unkind about them. He said once: 'Why are the British always going on about bloody nurses?' But on the whole he was their champion.

'The babies are really the most remarkable of all. One can hardly believe that those squat featureless objects bear any resemblance to a human infant – and, in fact, I remember that a mother once angrily contested the point.

'Giles fans rushed their babies' photographs to the *Daily Express*, which printed them in a row beside the corresponding Giles drawing. The result was a triumphant vindication of his art.

'Great cartoonists fulfil a role similar to that of the ancient court jester, wrapping the truth in clothing of humour to make it palatable.

'Giles does much the same thing.

'Although we love the situations and captions of his cartoons, they are not really so important as his superb revelation of our absurdity.

This photograph shows Giles having just emerged from East Suffolk and Ipswich Hospital where he had been treated for blood poisoning. He had punctured a finger with a drawing pin. Giles is seen with three of the nurses and a ward sister who looked after him. One could say he was in his element.

our cat

mr giles saying o.

dear editor,

as the youngest and only member of the giles famly who knows where the pen is i am writing to say he is sorry he cant send a cartoon this week as he is in hospital with blud poyson.

he says the nurses are all very nice and keep sticking ~~penny pensil~~ penicilin in im and eury time he says o we all laugh. ~~he says the doctors are a lot of~~ the doctors are also very nice and all look very fit. so are all the visitors who keep bringing him flours and smoking his cigeretts. he likes it ever so much in hospital and only has to have fairly light chains to hold him down now. he arsks me to say that the fact that he only drinks ~~penny pensil~~ penicilin these days, and the fact that wisky sales have dropped is purely a coincidence and hopes he will be back soon.

←flours.

Sunday Express, Sept. 4th, 1955

George Junior sometimes stands in for Giles when he is indisposed. Here is a letter to the Editor, apologising for the lack of a cartoon.

148

'Went head over heels giving One an extra special curtsy'   *Sunday Express, Sept. 2nd, 1990*

This cartoon refers to Prince Charles' visit to hospital following his nasty polo injury. The nurse in the doorway is worth studying for her justifiable look of indignation.

'I appreciate the desire to witness the second half of the World Cup, but I would prefer the choir not to leave at the trot.'

Sunday Express, June 21st, 1970

In June 1970, West Germany beat England 3–2 in Mexico, knocking them out of the World Cup. Note the grotesquely ugly little bruiser running alongside the bespectacled child who could well be a young Giles. He surely must be someone the artist knows. Notice, too, that none of the little perishers' feet are touching the ground.

VE-DAY 1945:
'Now it's over, I'll get some leave and repair that gutter and put a couple of boards in that fence.'

VE-DAY 1985

Sunday Express, May 5th, 1985

DIY conscious Giles seems suddenly to have taken an objection to the state, on the fortieth anniversary of VE-day, of the Family's suburban home.

'When I asked you where you would be putting your cross I was asking a perfectly civil question.'

Sunday Express, April 15th, 1979

Giles would not be able to conceive of anything more irritating than being pestered by a canvassing MP while attending to his boat. The cartoonist's own boats, over the years, were magnificent craft compared with this one. But Giles had a great bond with all those who loved boats and the sea.

'Lady, you don't happen to have one about horses being unfair to riders?'

Daily Express, April 30th, 1974

Giles also loved horses and was himself a skilled horseman who had once given professional lessons. Still, he was always irritated by what he regarded as unnecessary sentimentality about animals. Note the leaping horse, like Nureyev, in the top left-hand corner of the cartoon.

'Let us all thank him for helping us to laugh at ourselves; it is the hardest lesson to learn and far the most valuable.'

Almost every tribute to Giles refers to his gentle nature and the love he has for the British. It was refreshing therefore to come across an old piece by Nathaniel Gubbins, a colleague of Carl's on the *Sunday Express*, who advanced a somewhat alternative point of

153

view. There may be a good deal more in what he says than those – almost everyone, indeed – who romanticise about Carl and what they like to view as his almost angelic nature.

Wrote Gubbins in the fifties: 'From Dean Swift to Giles the men who have made you laugh most have been savage men.

'Thoughtless people have lumped them all together under the title, humourist, which would include knockabout comedians, jugglers and clowns.

'But the laughter-makers who have been remembered, and who will be remembered in the years to come, are the satirists – the men who hate.

'Among the things they hate are stupidity, injustice, intolerance. If they have suffered from any of these, or all, so much the better for their art.

'This hatred, combined with a possibly subconscious desire for perfection in an imperfect world, produced men like Giles.

'I don't know what it is that Giles hates most. Maybe it's ugly and wicked children. Maybe it's hunting squires and hard-riding women. Maybe it's ancient aunts in hideous hats who always arrive for Christmas, or whenever there's a picnic or a free holiday.

'Whichever it is, cartoonist Giles has had his revenge on them all.'

CHAPTER FIVE

At Home in Suffolk

A spring day in 1992. Joan was guiding Carl in his wheelchair towards the sitting room door in the farmhouse when Butch the Airedale, who had been characteristically comatose, suddenly reacted to the knock of a tradesman. He hurled himself towards the kitchen, spinning the wheelchair and taking with him the flex to the telephone. The phone became airborne, flying to the length of its cord.

Teacups leapt from their saucers and a tin tray lifted from the trolley. Everything was suspended for a fraction of a second – caught and frozen for a frame, as in a Giles cartoon – and then, as if released, clattered and crashed to the floor amidst Carl's curses.

His alarm was understandable. In the previous eighteen months Carl, who had long suffered circulation problems, had had both legs amputated beneath the

Giles.

knee. Although he was hoping that he would grow strong enough with therapy to be fitted with artificial limbs he was forced, for the time being, to remain helpless in a wheelchair. He would be placed there in the morning and there he would stay, brightly dressed in a striped shirt and yellow V-necked jumper, with a tartan rug over his lap. Each day he was attended by nurses and regularly visited by his surgeon.

However, the inconvenience of his circumstances neither restricted his lunchtime jaunts to the tavern nor, when in good spirits, his good humour. One thing that did set him in a rage was the lack of understanding – by man or beast – of his physical vulnerability, the fact that one bang on either of the tender ends of his foreshortened legs, which stuck like unwilling buffers beyond the leading edge of the wheelchair, was unspeakable agony.

And so it was that Butch's rampage on that particular morning had unsettled him somewhat. Later, he was in a favourite position at the open French windows, looking out over trim grass sprinkled with the confetti scattering of blossom, when suddenly he scowled at distant movement on his lawn. 'The buggers,' he raged. 'Look at the buggers. JOAN, get my gun. The bastards. I'll get 'em.' Carl had spotted three rabbits hopping about feeding on his grass.

No gun was forthcoming. Something else caught Carl's attention. 'The little bastards – look at them.' On this occasion it was a couple of magpies which were taking a close interest in the chicken run. 'Joan – my gun.'

No gun came.

Carl seems to favour all-out war on small creatures. It is, at times, disconcerting, not least the attempt to film a duck walking across Fleet Street, which resulted in a number of fatalities. While work on *The Ugly Duckling* was still in progress, Carl was visited at the farmhouse by his editor Arthur Christiansen and Christiansen's wife, Brenda. The latter asked how it was that Carl managed to keep the ducks so still for the filming.

'I break their legs,' said Carl mischievously. Brenda looked appalled.

Carl's apparent callousness, some might feel, is reflected in his work. After all, his nasty little children are frequently abusing animals. So, is he cruel?

'No, he's not cruel,' says his friend Michael Bentine. 'Not a bit of it. He just tells these stories to shock. It's slightly dark humour. He didn't really break a duck's

Giles, when still fit and mobile, walks up the drive of Hillbrow Farm with Joan. Butch leads. The house is cheerful and brightly painted. It was transformed by Giles himself from a poky, gloomy seventeenth-century farmhouse into a cheerful, welcoming home. The furniture within is modern but comfortable. Everywhere there are games and toys. But no children, of course; the diversions are strictly for grown-ups. Round the corner to the right, incidentally, there is an old mangle. It is not the one, insists Giles, through which he wound all sister Eileen's teddy bears and golliwogs.

156

'Look at it this way, lady—with a couple of these in your garden there's less chance of them turning your place into an airfield.'

Sunday Express, May 14th, 1967

A double line of pylons, during the mid-sixties, came stomping over the horizon like those Martian machines in H.G. Wells' War of the Worlds *and right across Hillbrow Farm. There they stand with their feet planted in one of Giles' meadows, a hundred yards from the house. Giles fought a fierce battle, but lost.*

'Yet it's us they tag "dirty".'

Daily Express, April 3rd, 1956

Giles had a piggery in the early days and enjoyed the beasts. He certainly regarded them as having a great deal more dignity than human beings, a point which this cartoon makes with some force.

legs; he just wanted to see the reaction when he said he did.'

Bentine was asked to explain the filming of ducks waddling under Number 73 buses.

'Did he do that?' asked the comedian, initially shrieking with manic laughter and then subsiding into shocked seriousness. 'Look, what you've got to understand about Carl is that he operates – or used to operate – a pig farm. He is a country-man. What he's reacting to is what he perceives as town people's view of the countryside. You know the kind of thing – 'ere Mrs Stapelly-Farmyard, you 'ave a nice cuppa kindly tea now and 'elp yerself to another piece of nithering cake. The plain fact is that country people are chicken-stranglers, horse-knackerers, pig-slaughterers and sheep throat-cutters.

'He's not really cruel, but he can't stand sentimentality about animals. He hates the idea that anyone would spend more on pet food for cats than they would on starving children. He loathes

Giles tends his pigs. They were days of austerity and pig farmers were allowed to keep only one pig at a time for themselves. When a man from the ministry came to check up he asked to see the pig which had been killed for home consumption. He eyed the two halves of carcass hanging in the larder. They were two halves of a pig all right. Both of them the left half. 'Funny sort of pigs you have here, Mr Giles,' he said.

the idea of pampered pets, but loves gun dogs. He likes the idea of animals behaving naturally, and in their natural habitat. If they have to be shot because they're being a ruddy nuisance, then that's it.'

Lord Cudlipp enjoys the notion of Carl as a farming man. He tells the story of the early days when there was still rationing and when farmers were restricted to only a limited amount of their 192own produce. One day a 'man from the ministry' came to visit Carl in order to check out his piggery arrangements.

Recalls Cudlipp: 'This chap looked around and didn't say very much and nodded and scratched his head. Farmers were only allowed one pig for them-selves and, of course, that pig would be cut in half – up from the crotch, you know the way they do it – and hung.

'This inspector asked to see their "one" pig. Joan showed him into the larder and there, hanging in the dim, cool light, were two halves of carcass.

'Later at the gate the man thanked Carl for showing him around and just before taking his leave remarked: "Everything seems to be fine. But I must say that you certainly breed some remarkable pigs, Mr Giles. That carcass hanging in your larder, for example. It's the first I've ever seen with four left trotters."'

Carl's farm no longer has pigs, but the arable acreage is run by a manager. The only animals are the dozen chickens which provide the Gileses with splendid free-range eggs.

Carl bought Hillbrow Farm in the village of Witnesham just after the war and immediately set about converting the seventeenth-century farmhouse from what Joan called a gloomy junk box to a bright, cheerful and practical home. The main house and outbuildings are white; the woodwork – doors and frames and ledges and so on – a lively blue or scarlet. The roofs are of brick-red pantiles, giving that pleasing wave pattern characteristic of East Anglia. In the double-entrance driveway there are two Edwardian lamp posts. There is a well-tended greenhouse to the left of the main house and the lawn spreads away behind to a chicken run, beyond which is meadow and thick woodland.

The outhouses include a couple of garages, a number of farm buildings and, most significant of all, Carl's workshop, a professionally equipped sixty-foot-long, well-lit building which more appropriately might be described as a private factory.

It is full of lathes of every description, a huge compressor, jigs and frames and sheets of metal and quality wood, row upon row of tools, each with a rack for its own category – countless chisels, for example, neatly graduating from the smallest to the largest, and a

OPPOSITE: *This is Giles in his workshop in 1952. His skills were endless: artist, musician, horseman, yachtsman, film-maker, racing driver, draughts champion, engineer and craftsman.*

magnificent collection of drill-bits. There is an enormous wall area of the kind of pigeon holes you find in the best ironmongers, full of nuts and bolts and screws and nails and joints and washers and tappets and gaskets and picture hooks and eyelets and what-have-you. Carl is equipped to build anything from a working/studio caravan, which he did, to an ocean-going liner, which he didn't. Carl, in dirty white overalls, would spend whole days absorbed and lost in this constructor's world, like a child in a giant Meccano set. Joan would visit him with sandwiches or a cup of tea and then fade away, unnoticed. Carl was not entirely unmolested, however.

When children were staying, their mothers would urge them, while Sunday lunch was being cooked, to 'go out and see what Uncle Carl is up to'. The little figures would go in and stand at a respectful distance and watch the engrossed figure bent over the workbench. Bit by bit, inch by inch, as in the game grandmother's footsteps, the kids would advance on Carl. He would only become aware of their presence when little pink fingers would rise from beneath and run back and forth, like creatures out of the sea, searching for nuts and bolts and interesting metal objects.

Carl claims he became impatient with this intrusion and that he successfully employed a simple deterrent. When he was welding, which was often, he would wear the sinister steel face-protector, in whose window was reflected the eerie blue flickering of intensely hot fire, and would from time to time simply run his oxyacetylene torch along the row of bolts and rivets which awaited his attention. They apparently glowed with what Carl called 'black heat'. When the little fingers seized these objects, there was a short and pitiful cry followed by the scamper of feet and distant wailing appeal for maternal aid.

As with many of Carl's rather more alarming stories, the listener is never quite sure to what extent there may exist an element of mischievous fantasy.

Giles in his favourite location – his workshop. Each tool is lovingly drawn.

Outside the workshop, you can wander among the other outhouses and sheds and peek through the odd pane of glass or through a crack in the wood. You would spot Carl's Bentley Mulsanne, dusty now and long unused; you might see his Jaguar XK120 which he raced at Silverstone, its tyres flat and now showing the occasional blisters of rust; you would spot his Range Rover and his Land Rover, the first ever sold. You might feel a little sad. Carl certainly does. 'I don't like to think of them too much,' he says.

These are adult toys of the most spectacular kind, but Carl may never again be able to play with them, to take them on the open road, to drive, as he did, with enormous speed and with his heart full of that indescribable motoring pleasure expressed by Toad of Toad Hall. Carl's not at all like the boastful Toad, but he does share the fellow's love of motor cars and luxury caravans and boats.

One day when Carl was visited by his friends comedian Eric Sykes and writer Johnny Speight, he asked that someone open his garage just before they arrived. He didn't say why, but it was clear that he wanted them to notice his Bentley. It was the kind of pride, touching under the circumstances, that a child might take in his bike, leaving it, casually, in a prominent position where it might be seen by his chums.

Toys of a simpler nature are in evidence all about the house. In the small front hall, stacked against a wall opposite the umbrellas, is one of those football games where the players are operated by rotating handles projecting from each side of a rectangular wooden tray. Stacked behind that is a shove-halfpenny board. One of the two adjacent living room areas is more of a bar and a playroom than a sitting room. There is a dartboard over the fireplace. Neatly positioned about the place, on ledges and in corners, are all manner of games and Dinky toys, little wind-up monkeys and clockwork clowns, jigsaws and Monopoly sets. There is a bar, with a mirror over it, built like a boat. It is as if Carl has cut

one side off the hull of a clinker-built yacht, stuck and bolted it against the wall in his sitting room and neatly arranged upon the lacquered deck a large collection of spirits and beverages.

It is towards this boat that any visitor is usually first directed, at any time of the day or night.

The immediate impression is of a playroom for grown-ups. Indeed everywhere there are the signs of active leisure, fun, parties, visitors, merriment. Yet, curiously, there is not the slightest feeling that this is a place for children.

'I've got thousands of nephews and nieces,' says Carl with some irritation.

'Actually, we've got two,' says Joan quietly.

One game, alone and easily accessible on a shelf, is an old draughts set, the corners of the cardboard box frayed and the battered lid, long warped and torn, a loose fit. Carl is a fanatical draughts player. He once won, it may be recalled, the school tournament. His trophy, offered in malevolent mockery by the frightening Mr Chalk, had been a useless tennis ball. But those few who knew about and respected such things regarded him as a Grand Master. He was to be feared. And rightly. For, among other things, he was of the classical school that insisted – and here is the true sign of the purist draughts player – on 'no huffing'.

Carl's principal partner and most stubborn challenger in these later years is a man called Louis, a twenty-stone, amiable scrap dealer and backyard Ipswich entrepreneur. Louis is also operator of a number of ageing Volvo taxis and became, particularly after Carl lost his legs, his unofficial chauffeur/companion. Louis is on priority call, on a daily and nightly basis, except for Saturdays. He will turn up as summoned, an always smiling, bespectacled giant of a figure for whom everything is 'loverly' and 'bootiful'. On greeting the Gileses at their front door, he will observe, even if it is raining: 'What a loverly day. My old dad used to like a day like this. Bootiful.' He will then wheel Carl to the side of the car. Carl's vulnerable legs miss door posts

'Which goes to prove that even if you don't think they're all little Florence Nightingales don't let them hear you say so.'

Sunday Express, July 11th, 1971

Giles is now confined to a wheelchair and has adapted to his circumstances with fortitude. Fortunately, such is his sense of humour that he would undoubtedly be the one to laugh the loudest at the irony of this particular cartoon.

'He does that every time British Rail put their fares up.'

Sunday Express, Nov. 24th, 1985

Poor old British Rail getting it again. The children's lack of alarm over this appalling act of destruction is astonishing.

and other obstructions by inches and by the time Carl arrives at the vehicle he will often have the pale resigned look of a medieval martyr, head slumped on one side and all emotion drained away by the overwhelming terror of the ordeal.

'Bootiful,' says Louis, not noticing the almost imperceptible flicker of deep irritation on his helpless friend's face.

Louis then bodily eases Carl from his wheelchair and slides him along a varnished wooden board into the passenger seat. 'You all right, Carl?' he keeps asking. 'That's bootiful.' Carl's leg-ends miss the window handle by a centimetre. 'Uh...ah...ooo...' is usually Carl's nervous response. To be fair to Louis, he does a splendid job and Carl, for all his moaning and grunting, is in good hands, but he never gives the impression of very much trust. When Carl is settled and before the door is slammed, Louis asks: 'You all right, Carl?' There is a grunt from within. 'Loverly,' Louis says. And – slam – Carl is shut in. 'Bootiful.'

Each day Carl and Louis would thus set forth at lunchtime, or less frequently in the evenings, to the taverns and old familiar waterside inns which they have both known for most of their lives.

A particular favourite is the Maybush, a pub on the estuary just outside Ipswich. It was outside this tavern that Carl's yacht used to be moored. Boats of all shapes and classes, pulled up into the adjacent yard, give authentic style to the place.

And from vessels dipping and swaying from their moorings outside the picture window of the saloon bar there is the constant slapping of halyards against aluminium masts, a background noise to put a jolly beat into every yachtsman's heart.

As Carl and Louis enter they come across a group, fresh from the sea, swigging jars of beer at the bar. There are men with beards and women with tousled hair and bright red cheeks and they all stand with their legs apart as if to counter a pitching deck. They wear polo-necked sweaters and have lanyards trailing from their pockets. They sport sailing wellies on their feet – deck boots – and their bright yellow oilskins squeak and hiss as they raise their pints.

It is not difficult to understand where Carl gathered the rich and often hilarious detail which brings to life his sailing cartoons. Indeed, there is a Giles cartoon on the wall of the Maybush, just inside the door, showing a hectic and chaotic regatta scene which is so full of activity that it takes a good twenty minutes to study.

''Ello, Carl, mate,' shouts a man whose face has been lashed crimson by endless Atlantic storms and whose wild, greying hair strays happily from round a burnished bald pate.

Carl, who is already ogling the barmaid, raises a hand in salutation.

Often Carl and Louis end their day at a rather garish nightclub in Ipswich, one of those places set back from the road with a semi-circle of different-coloured lightbulbs summoning the fun-seekers. It is called, wonderfully, the Chevalier Club. You might expect a Frenchman in a straw hat to be the main attraction.

But it isn't that sort of a place. Carl and Louis, usually half deafened by the resident discotheque, 'shoot pool' there. Well after midnight they return home and settle down to a couple of serious hours of draughts. Joan, in dressing gown, provides the sausages.

The extraordinary Louis is also an employer of some local note. He lives in the middle of Ipswich in an old, many-roomed mansion with a belfry, which was once the home of the aristocratic Cobbold family. It is now surrounded by a large area of wasteland which Carl describes as looking like a huge sandpit.

Here and there in these now derelict stately acres are funny little sheds surrounded by dumps and rubbish piles and bits of cars.

'You know something about Louis,' says Carl, adjusting himself in his wheelchair by the French windows at Hillbrow Farm. 'He says he's a second-hand car dealer. Bugger that. He's a scrap metal merchant. Most of his cars come out square.'

I must go down to the sea again, to the lonely sea and the sky...

Sunday Express, July 20th, 1952

This cartoon features the Maybush Inn near Ipswich. The waterside pub has for a long time been a favourite of Giles. It is often full of sailing types in oilskins and rubber boots. They drink manly pints, tell seafaring tales and tend to stand about with their legs slightly apart as if bracing themselves against the heaving of a deck.

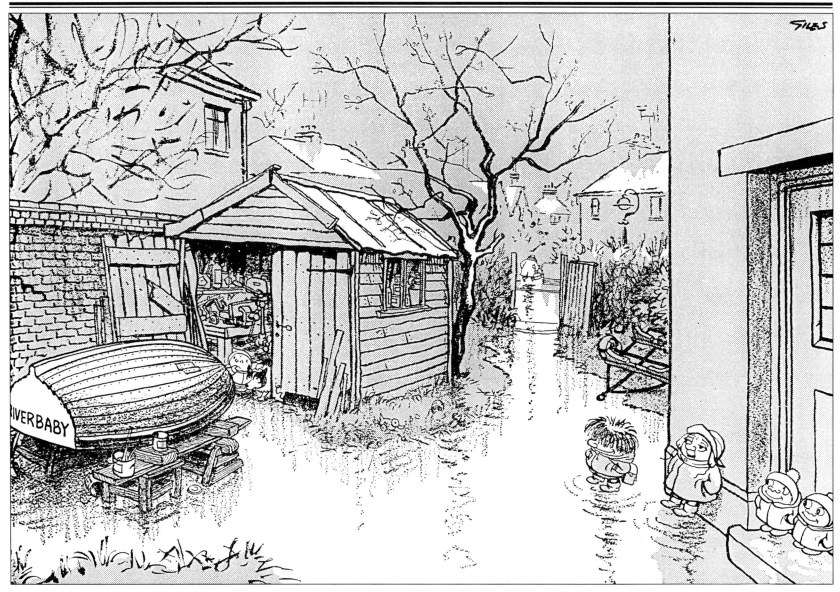

'He spent all his holiday painting the name on his boat—I hadn't the heart to tell him.'

Daily Express, April 12th, 1966

As boating disasters go, this is not the most serious. But it is pretty devastating just the same. Note Father in the distance going off to work, contented that he is now ready to go to sea.

'With crews like mine, no wonder they sail round the world single-handed.'

Daily Express, Sept. 5th, 1977

Giles was a very good sailor but he often witnessed the appalling incompetence which is so familiar in family yachting.

Louis has, in fact, about six separate businesses of different kinds, mostly run by curious raggedy chums of his, some of them tramps or eccentrics, and all forming part of his chain of interests. Carl knew these chaps well and describes them as like that ragged band of friends of the Hunchback of Notre Dame, who used to lurk in the shadows of the cathedral and beneath the archways of the bridges over the Seine.

One of Louis' 'chief mechanics' is Tom Champion. Tom is deaf and dumb and has a wooden leg. Another is 'Crabapple' Billy. And another is 'Peasenhall' Bob. Then there is 'Mad' Monty who is always 'setting fire to

'Some of these entries in your diary had better be fakes, my lady.'

Sunday Express, May 8th, 1983

The Sunday Times *and leading historian Lord Dacre, formerly Hugh Trevor-Roper, were hoaxed by history's most clever and, in the end, most hilarious literary forgery, the Hitler diaries. The world had seldom had such a laugh at the newspaper industry. The* Times *was said to have paid £1 million for them.*

things'. And 'Lofty', a chap who is like an ostrich and whom Louis used to find, during his late evening rounds, literally hanging by his arms on a high fence, his feet clear of the ground. 'You all right?' Louis would ask. 'I'm all right, boy,' Lofty would reply. 'Loverly, bootiful,' Louis would say and move off into the darkness.

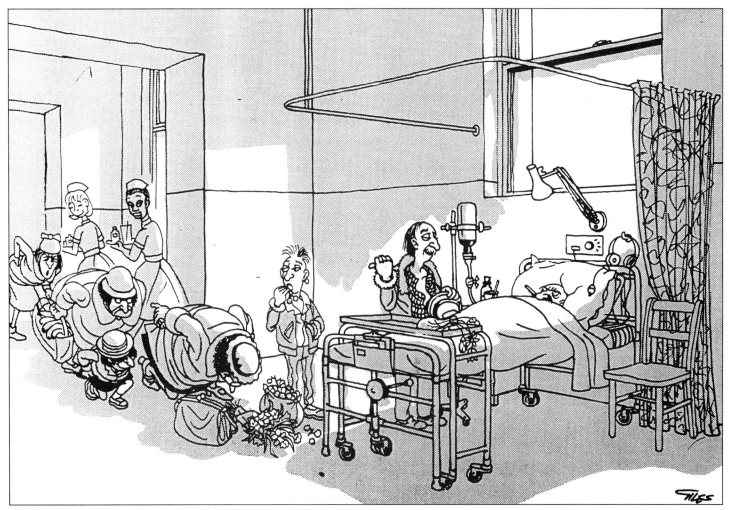

'The curtsy is in case you got a drop of Prince Charles's blood in yer.'

Sunday Express, March 3rd, 1985

This is one 'royal' cartoon whose original was not requested by the member of the family involved. Perhaps Prince Charles, who had become a donor, felt that such a thing was no laughing matter. Perhaps it made him realise, all of a sudden, that royal blood might be ending up in unsuitable veins.

171

Here, Giles, as President of the British Cartoonists' Association, is seen with Princess Margaret at an exhibition of newspaper cartoon art in 1970.

EPSOM

Grandma, in a more recent cartoon, at Epsom on Derby Day. The old girl went to terrifying extremes to guarantee the success of her chosen horses. And her own ability to ride might have come as a surprise to many.

'With Christmas shoppers in mind don't you think you might try something in the Constable style?'

Sunday Express, Nov. 23rd, 1986

Giles returns to his Bohemian attic.

'Come in Corporal—we have a Mrs McGinty who insists that even if we're leaving Ireland
YOU'RE staying here!'

Daily Express, Feb. 10th, 1987

There have never been many laughs in the Ulster situation for Giles or anyone else. He makes an exception in this case. Apart from the graffiti, the scenes of destruction in the background could almost be France in 1945. But note how his soldiers have changed with the times, even to the longer hair worn by the officer.

But it is old Tom who seems to provide Carl with the greatest pleasure. 'He is like Long John Silver and used to wear an old captain's hat,' he says. 'He is on a disability pension. But he could do all kinds of things. He was an archery champion and gun-club champion. He is very clever.'

Tom took to wearing a cheap black wig. He had hired it. With his sea-captain's headgear and his wig and his fine profile he looked as fetching as Errol Flynn. The trouble was that he failed to keep up the £2-a-week payments on his wig and was faced, inevitably, with the day of reckoning. The wig man paid a call on Tom and a witness recalled that the two men were not many minutes in discussion when the wig man suddenly ran out of Tom's door with a look of terror on his face, shouting wildly: 'The man's mad. The man's mad.' Tom, it transpired, had hit the fellow on the head with a stick. The wig man ran off and was not seen again. As for the wig itself, Tom's still wearing it.

Tom, for some other reason, remembers Carl, found himself before the local magistrate. Since he is deaf and dumb he had required that an expert in sign language be present to interpret.

Half way through the hearing Tom complained that he was unable to understand the deaf and dumb sign-language person. Why was that, he was asked from the bench. 'Well, he's from London,' indicated Tom with a flurry of indignant signalling. The case was dismissed.

These were – and are – the characters who quite genuinely occupy Carl's natural world. Through the years he would put on a smart suit, just occasionally, and go to London to see Lord Beaverbrook, famous journalists or the Queen. But, above all, he loved the Toms and the Loftys and the 'Mad' Harrys and Eddie 'The Pig Man', and so on. And Louis, of course.

OPPOSITE: *Giles, a fine horseman, is seen here photographed by the Daily Express in 1952 in order to publicise the fact that he was about to cover – in cartoon – the Flat season.*

Louis tells of one early morning when he and Carl had emerged from the Chevalier. A number of other members had staggered off into the darkness while Carl had positioned himself with his wrists and ankles poking through the white picket fence which ran either side of the establishment's front gate. Carl laid his head between two of the pointed post-tops so that it looked as if he were in the stocks.

A passing taxi drew up briefly, its headlights shining directly at Carl. 'Who's that?' the taxi driver called over to Louis.

'That's Mr Giles,' replied Louis.

'Who's Mr Giles?' asked the cabbie.

'You know, Giles,' called Louis.

'Oh, Giles,' said the taxi driver, suddenly astonished. ''Ere, you know who that is?' he said to his passengers. 'That's Giles.' As the cab drew away, the wide-eyed couple turned round and surveyed the figure until they had turned a corner into central Ipswich.

Carl's sister Eileen, who lives not far from Witnesham with her retired husband, has come to tea. She places a hand on Carl's shoulder, surprising him. He looks round, his poor eyesight always causing half a second's delay, and then grins with pleasure. 'Hello, mate,' he says.

Eileen is an attractive lady with smartly cropped, boy-length white hair and a quietly stylish sense of dress. She smiles a lot, seems to be a happy woman, and like all the other females in Carl's life has such a deep affection for the man that she is prepared to put up with practically anything; although, like Joan, she is not beyond quietly asserting herself when matters get out of hand.

Carl will be cheerful and amusing for an agreeable period of time and will then, without much warning, take objection to something or someone with great vigour. It is always a disruptive business and the gathering has to adjust itself to deal with the matter as best it can.

'Mr. Stevens felt chilly—his gas fire went out.'

Daily Express, Feb. 15th, 1973

Bedrooms were seldom places of tranquillity in Giles' suburbia. Often, as in the first of two drawings, they were the scenes of the most terrible crises. We laugh at the situation, but it is difficult to imagine that this drama could end in anything but the most unspeakable catastrophe.

**'Awake, O Lord of the Manor, 'tis Father's Day and thou shalt do no work all day.
Just like the other 51 Sundays in the year.'**

Sunday Express, June 19th, 1966

This second bedroom scene is far less serious. But hardly peaceful. We must assume that the twins are about to fire real rifles, otherwise there wouldn't be much point. Giles seemed to be intrigued by both Mother's and Father's Days. They were anniversaries, so it seemed to him, devised in hell.

'Bertie never thought about this sort of thing until he saw Mary Whitehouse's anti-porn film.'

Daily Express, Feb. 19th, 1987

Mary Whitehouse's anti-pornography campaign involved her going round the country showing a quite shocking film, a collection of scenes depicting sex and violence, to journalists and MPs. She packed them in.

On this April afternoon Carl suddenly, and surprisingly, attacks the nursing profession. 'What is it about the British, always going on about nurses – they're useless half the time,' he rages from his wheelchair by the French window.

'They've done a lot for you, Carl,' Eileen says.

'Done what for me? What do you know? You're all the same. Women. Bloody nurses, you'd think they were all without fault...'

There seems to be no particular reason for this assault on the angels, but it is a good, emotive subject, likely to get people into a state and, anyway, Carl is still mildly out of sorts following the incident with Butch and one thing and another.

Tea has arrived on a trolley. There are confections of all kinds: Battenburg cake, chocolate cake, various biscuits and a summer pudding with an attendant jug of thick cream. Carl has a special table which slides over his lap until it is gently touching his tummy just below his rib cage. It is a perfect platform/tray, easy to put in place, easy to move away. On this occasion the rounded corner of the thing, as Joan slides it over Carl's knees, prods him, quite gently, just above the solar plexus. Carl shouts with plainly bogus agony. Joan steps back a pace. 'Kah, what are you bloody well doing, woman? Trying to kill me? Did you see that?' he enquires of a slightly embarrassed male guest, a figure reluctant to become a party to this drama. 'See what I mean about nurses?'

'It hardly touched you,' complains Joan.

'Honestly, Carl,' says Eileen, who cannot help smiling at the absurdity.

'Watch it or you'll get a good thumping,' glowers Carl at his kid sister.

'Thank God you weren't a soldier,' says Joan, feeling brave enough to complete the adjustment of the table.

'Kah,' goes Carl again. 'Kah, would you believe it?'

'Do you want me to pour this over your head?' asks Joan sweetly, picking up the jug of thick cream.

By now Carl is smiling broadly, but he will not yet drop the subject. 'Amazin', isn't it?' his Cockney suddenly evident. 'All she has to do is push a table gently in front of me and she has to go whacking me in the solar plexus, knockin' all the wind out of me.' Carl's male friend offers a noncommittal shrug. Joan's hand reaches again for the cream.

'Honestly,' says Eileen, sipping her tea. 'What a fuss.'

'You watch it, mate,' says Carl pointing a teaspoon at her. 'Just remember that you're under the same contract now as you were when you were two.'

Eileen fails to look particularly frightened, but it is clear that she remembers the terrors of sixty-five years ago with no difficulty at all.

She recalls for everyone's benefit how she and Carl would be sent to do the shopping. On the way home Carl would throw the carrier bags and packages of meat and sausages into any garden where there appeared to be a fierce dog. Eileen, on each occasion, would bravely retrieve the purchases, often just clearing a wall or privet hedge before the slavering jaws nabbed her posterior. Carl is amused by the recollections. His love for Eileen, regardless of the evidence, is total. He has, as far as one can tell, spent a happy life putting all of those he loves, particularly the women, to regular and exquisite torture.

Still, in the story of the Giles family, with all of its branches supporting uncles and aunts and nephews and nieces and relatives near and far, there is no suggestion of genuine acrimony whatsoever. It would be almost impossible to find another family where there was not, in at least one unpleasant little quarter, a dark story of bitterness and hatred. You won't find it here.

Carl can be short-tempered, impatient, unreasonable and, on occasions, absurdly intolerant and self-indulgently hostile, but he is a man with an immense and generous capacity for love. He may not show it very well, for he is not a demonstrative man in that sense. But he has a deep, natural affection for those people who have proved their worth; he has a deep love for the best in mankind and, at moments when he is able to overcome his uncomfortable inclination towards atheism, a profound desire for faith.

'I would just so love there to be a God,' he says, in an astonishing moment. 'So that I could have someone to thank. There is so much to be thankful for.'

The more you get to know Carl the less unsettled you become by his crotchety outbursts. There is no doubt that he can make life difficult – at times very difficult indeed – but the main feature of his petulant rages is the fact that they last, on the whole, only a very short period of time and never appear to have any great substance, aftermath or permanent effect. They are like the sudden, brisk spring showers which that afternoon chased across the Giles farmstead. One moment the rain and hail were driving against the sitting room picture window and splashing up from the steps down to the lawn and the next the sun was shining and the rabbits, briefly frightened off by the hailstones, were back nibbling at the edge of the flowerbed. So it was with Carl.

'See those woods down there,' he said, nurses and incompetent women forgotten, pointing to the dark forest across his fields. 'I sit here and imagine what goes on. Everyone's at it down there. Local husbands with other people's wives, young girls – probably underage – with the lads from the village. All of them at it. You can't see a thing. Look how still it is. You go down there – then you'll see 'em. In the undergrowth – everywhere. At it.

'You know that big corn field over the lane. Well, once, before it was harvested, I saw this young pair, hand in hand, walking bold as anything right through the middle of the crop. So I shouted, "'Ere, you two!" You know what happened? A dozen couples stood up.'

A dozen? Well, it was probably three or four. But then Carl sees everything as a cartoon. His embellishments are the gifts which the artist, especially the humorous one, must always be allowed to bestow; the rearranging of life a little to give a more amusing pattern to things.

A cartoon which captures much of Carl's life and adventures in Suffolk shows a number of yachtsmen in a couple of car-towed dinghies pursued by the police. The sailors are all hanging out as ballast, in the familiar style, to prevent their craft from keeling over. The police in the police car – note the vintage – are doing the same.

Carl likes this picture. It's all there, really. The exhilaration of the highway, the boats, the fun, summer – the police in full chase.

Carl was a highly responsible sailor, much respected by his peers, but on the road he liked speed. He was a good driver, but fast.

The police would often be dozing in some rural East Anglian lay-by when there would be a rush and a roar and a blur of expensive metal. The police would adjust their caps and set off in pursuit.

Some time later the face of the law, all screwed up with mock concern and long-suffering anguish, would appear at the window of Carl's latest high-performance possession.

''Ello, Mr Giles, in a hurry to get our cartoon to the train again, are we? Got to catch our deadline, 'ave we?'

Things were no different, curiously enough, when Carl took Joan, at the generous no-expense-spared invitation of Lord Beaverbrook, on their first trip to the United States. It was in 1948. The jaunt was to be a driving visit, covering America coast to coast, during which Carl would send back cartoons of his impressions.

America, for Carl, was simply a movie come to life. The police, in particular, were so like the figures that he had seen in the cinema, looking and behaving in entirely the same way and using the same script, that he found it difficult to take them seriously. In any case, he was to get to know them quite well.

He recalls one particular encounter in the Midwest when he had driven straight across a main intersection. He managed to avoid colliding with the huge pounding trucks but was spotted by the Highway Patrol.

This is a wonderfully surreal drawing which shows a combination of the pursuits which Giles loved best, motoring, sailing and keeping the constabulary on its toes.

Giles with a young Stirling Moss at Silverstone. He raced his own Jaguar XK120 there.

'This bike came up in my rearview mirror with its siren going and a light flashing,' recalls Carl. 'The policeman got off very slowly and walked to my car. He was one of those with a cowboy hat on. He leaned down and looked at me in a good-humoured kind of way, took his hat off and scratched his head slowly and thoughtfully with the same hand. After quite a long while of studying me he said: "D'you know, sir, that you just went through a stop sign?"

'I hadn't seen any stop sign. The trouble is that their signs are little round things, like saucers, at the top of a very high pole. I don't know how anyone sees them.

'I said to the policeman: "I didn't see any sign." He said: "Will you come this way, sir?" So the two of us crossed this six-lane highway to get to the sign on the other side. It took us ages, with all this heavy traffic going by. When we got to the other side we both squinted up at the top of this great, long pole.

'The policeman asked me: "Can you see anything up there?" I said: "Well, I can see a little sign, but not even you could read that." He didn't say anything and we walked all the way back across the highway to the car. As he was writing out the summons he said: "Now, you will remember that sign, won't you, sir?" He must have thought that I looked doubtful, because he gestured to me with his index finger and we did the whole thing again, walked across this great interstate highway and back to the post with the little sign. "See that sign up there?" he asked me. "Yes," I said. "Can you read it, sir?" "Yes," I said. We then walked all the way back to the car again. Joan had just been sitting there.'

Back in Suffolk, the police were not always quite so patient, though the relationship was, taken in the broader view, always a friendly one. The generosity of the funds following many a policemen's ball often had more than a little to do with Carl.

The police did attend one incident, however, which was certainly very short on laughs. On this occasion, in the late fifties, Carl was not the driver. He was sitting in the back of a Ford Anglia driven by his dear friend of the time, Clifford Clarke, a tailor from Ipswich.

The car failed to negotiate a country corner, mounted the bank, just missing a tree, and then rolled back onto the road where it came to rest, steam hissing from the radiator and bits of metal tinkling from the crumpled bodywork. Carl slowly untangled himself in the back seat, testing his limbs for full movement and tenderly touching other vital areas for signs of damage. He gradually became aware of a stickiness at the back of his head and delicately probed the area with his fingers. To his horror he found that they sank into a warm mush, within which he could detect small sharp fragments, loose and moving slowly about in the goo. Carl knew that what he was feeling was skull and brain. He waited for greyness to envelope him. There was no pain. But this was it. Oblivion.

Carl was spared. For what had happened was that the back of his head had smashed into a paper bag full of a dozen eggs, from Carl's own chickens, which friend Cliff had put on the ledge by the back window. Much merriment followed, though there was nothing funny about the state of Cliff's car. It was a write-off.

Cliff, among them all – tramps, lunatics, comedians and peers of the realm – was Carl's very best chum. He ran his own tailor's business in Ipswich. He was a steady, kind, unremarkable man, and Carl liked him for his total honesty, for his lack of side and malice, for his ability to appreciate the hilarious nonsense of life. He laughed hugely at Carl, he found him to be the funniest and most engaging man he had ever encountered. Carl, of course, liked that, but he particularly appreciated the compliment because it came from such a fundamentally ordinary and decent man. It was a powerful friendship and Carl was greatly distressed when Cliff died.

Cliff, the Ipswich tailor, was the closest, the dearest of Carl's friends. Louis, particularly latterly, is the good-natured companion, driver and draughts opponent. Crazy Tom and the rest are the 'rude mechanicals', like the colourful crowd of merry misfits who attended Shakespeare's convivial taverner, Falstaff,

'It's the dawn chorus of smokers' coughs I shall miss most.'

Sunday Express, March 8th, 1987

Giles smoked all of his life until more recent years. He was once caught by Chalkie with a tin of fake cigarettes, a display item from his father's shop in the Barbican.

**'How do they tie "Bring us our bows, arrers, spears, chariots of fire"
with the peace talks in Stockholm?'**

Daily Express, Sept. 23rd, 1986

*Chalkie, even above the din, has spotted the boy who is talking. There will be terrible trouble when Chalkie sees the
note on the pianist's backside.*

a somewhat fatter figure than Carl but with much of the same spirit, grouchy and full of hilarity by turns.

But there are also, in curious contrast, the celebrities who regularly used to arrive at Hillbrow Farm, the newspaper editors, tycoons, occasionally Prince Charles waiting in an idling helicopter for Carl to join him for a luncheon, and, most significantly, professional men of comedy. The closest of these are Alf Garnett's creator, Johnny Speight, comedian and script-writer Eric Sykes, former 'Goon Show' founder, Michael Bentine and the late incomparable Tommy Cooper.

'I would always go and meet them at Ipswich station,' says Carl. 'I remember Tommy Cooper would get off the train onto the empty platform – this awkward figure that you always imagined with his magician's fez on – and as he passed the ticket office he would give the ticket inspector this extra long look. The poor little man sitting there with his specs wouldn't know what had happened to him.'

Joan would lay on the customary feast, usually having to wait well beyond the appointed hour for Carl and his friends to complete the essential pre-lunch pub crawl, and the farmhouse would shout with laughter well into the evening.

Recalls Eric Sykes: 'Train times would come and go and Carl would do everything he could to keep you there. We would usually stagger out and just catch the last train back to Liverpool Street.'

Carl's friendship with Michael Bentine was based partly on their mutual love of sailing. Says Bentine: 'He was a brilliant sailor and I was useless. But we used to really do it properly. He just had that same magical feeling about yachts and boats and barges. We loved the mystique of it all. We weren't the sort of yachting people who shouted out "Hello, there, ahoy, what a spanking good breeze," we really sailed the bloody things.'

There were lighter moments. They once collected a vicar from Felixstowe in order to sail him to a 'blessing of the assembled boats' up the River Deben. The vicar stood on the prow as they progressed along the coast, his surplice flapping in the relentless offshore breeze like an untethered spinnaker. Powerful beverages were handed up to him from the galley and a number of shoreside alehouses were visited on the way.

By the time the parson had been delivered to his bobbing congregation he was – and here the phrase is apt – three sheets to the wind. He swayed about on the prow, his raised hand attempting to give the sturdy sign of the cross, as if he were about to plunge into the deep.

Occasionally, back in London, the shirt-sleeved executives at the *Daily* or *Sunday Express* would be concerned about some detail of a cartoon. They would call the farmhouse only to be told that Carl was 'at sea'. Coastal pubs would be alerted and a watch would be kept through binoculars for Carl's vessel. It would eventually be spotted and a person with a loud-hailer would stand on the shore and bellow: 'Carl, could you please call the *Daily Express*.' There would be much cursing from Carl and he would nudge his vessel alongside at the nearest convenient landing point in order to deal with some hateful newspaper official who had probably never seen a yacht from closer than a cable's length.

'I really don't know him all that well,' says Bentine. 'He's an elusive character. Well, of course he's crotchety, all artists are. I think of him as one of the most straightforward, honest, modest men I've ever met. But the most striking thing about him, and the thing I adore him for, is his profound and never ceasing love of humour and the ridiculous. How could you not feel deeply for a man who sees the whole of our existence, particularly this very peculiar and unique British kind of existence, as something which is endlessly and gloriously funny and absurd?

OPPOSITE; *In October 1987, Giles strolls with his Airedale, Butch, near Hillbrow Farm. His slightly imperious look is quite out of character. He doesn't like cameras.*

189

'Of course he's a ruddy genius. Has any artist ever caught the British so accurately and with such a mixture of mischief, good nature and compassion?'

Carl sits at his French windows considering it all. He is a man who, on constant reflection, regards the whole of his life as being gloriously happy. He has no complaints, no regrets at all.

'That was such a happy time,' he says, recalling the wartime days of his black GI friends and the jazz band they formed at the Fountain pub, just down the road.

Of his and Joan's trip to America he says: 'What good times they were.' Of his experiences as an animator for the great Alexander Korda in the late twenties, he says: 'What an honour it was and what fun we had.' Remembering pre-war *Reynolds News* days and, thereafter, his fifty years with the *Daily Express*, he recalls: 'So much laughter.' Of his motoring and yachting and DIYing and film-making and partying and pubbing and roistering, he declares: 'Marvellous.'

Joan, pouring the tea, looks at him briefly and says: 'You're always saying that.'

'Well, that's how it was,' says Carl.

It is now morning. The showers have gone and it is a beautiful spring day at Hillbrow Farm. Carl is back by the French windows, tartan rug over his lap. He squints into the sun, irritated perhaps by a rabbit which is heading for his flowerbed.

Butch is lying a few feet away regarding his master with one half-open eye. A field mouse, unseen to most, is assessing the morning through its front door, paw on hip, with spring-cleaning on its mind. A carrion crow on high, hunched and horrible, peers down at this breakfast morsel.

Joan has served coffee. There is a knock on the door. It heralds the daily appearance of an attractive lady with a starched collar, a breezy smile and a thermometer in her bosom pocket. Her predecessors, for some fifty years, have been starring in the best of Giles' cartoons.

'You'll have to excuse me for a moment,' says Carl, grinning impishly at the small gathering. 'The nurse has arrived. She's come to wash my winkle.'

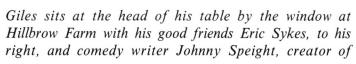

Giles sits at the head of his table by the window at Hillbrow Farm with his good friends Eric Sykes, to his right, and comedy writer Johnny Speight, creator of Cockney bigot, Alf Garnett. The remains of one of Joan's feasts lie on the table. It has been the usual happy lunch. The tiles have lifted to the laughter.

190

'What an escape from the Gulf crisis—watching Chalkie on holiday!'

A final look at them all. Grandma is following up the rear, Vera's snivelling, the twins are airborne down the steps and look who's about to sit back in his deckchair.

'It's the plumber we ordered in August—he can come and do the drain this afternoon.'

Daily Express, Dec. 24th, 1982